Advance Praise for *Performing Communities*

It's not as if our politicians are doing such a great job – why not turn to artists, playwrights, and actors to show us how to challenge and change our world? Where we live – on intimate, local ground – is where these ensemble theaters make their stand, but their impact, as much needed models for action, is global in scope.

Suzanne Lacy, artist and educator
Otis College of Art and Design, Los Angeles

For those of us in the contemporary ensemble field it's exhilarating to read histories that speak to the passions, the challenges, the vision of artists whose shoulders we stand amidst and upon. Their voices and the commentaries this book provide are a great resource for practitioners, teachers and students. Anyone with an interest in art making and democracy today will find it invaluable.

Michael Rohd
Sojourn Theatre, Portland, Oregon

U.S. ensemble theater's histories have not had the consistent scholarship that is needed to record, share or expand on a unique method of collective artistic expression and, hence, this publication does much to serve as a timely and valuable resource.

Angie Kim
Getty Foundation

It's great to hear the voices of so many artists and their community partners in crime! There's an in-the-trenches intimacy here that is missing from so much writing about community-based art. This is exciting new stuff that really digs deep at how art can engage and embolden the world around us.

Tim Miller, performer
Venice, California

i

PERFORMING COMMUNITIES

Grassroots Ensemble Theaters
Deeply Rooted in Eight U.S. Communities

Robert H. Leonard and Ann Kilkelly

Introduction by Jan Cohen-Cruz

Edited by Linda Frye Burnham

A project of the Community Arts Network

New Village Press
Oakland, California

Performing Communities: Grassroots Ensemble Theaters Deeply Rooted in Eight U.S. Communities

Printed in Canada.
First printing, April 2006.

The text of this book is printed on New Leaf EcoBook 50, an acid-free, recycled paper made of 50% post consumer waste. No chlorine bleach has been used to produce this paper.

Paperback
10-digit ISBN: 0-9766054-4-9
13-digit ISBN: 978-0-9766054-4-7

Library of Congress Control Number: 2006920582

To order copies of this book directly from the publisher please add US $5.00 shipping to the price of the book (for additional copies add $2.00/each). California residents add appropriate state sales tax. Send check or money order to New Village Press.

New Village Press
P.O. Box 3049
Oakland, CA 94609
(510) 420-1361
press@newvillage.net
www.newvillagepress.net

New Village Press books are published under the auspices of Architects/Designers/Planners for Social Responsibility.
www.adpsr.org

On the front cover:

"Parada da Rua," a community performance by Brazil's LUME, who brought the event to Dell'Arte International's Mad River Festival in Blue Lake, California, in 2000. Photo by Joan Schirle.

César Rodríguez of Teatro Pregones in "Fables of the Caribbean" (1994). Photo by Ricky Flores

On the back cover:

Emilia My Sumelius and Stephen Buescher in "Paradise Lost: Sacred Land," adapted and directed by Giulio Cesare Perrone with the Dell'Arte Company. Photo: Julia Puranen

Cover design by Lynne Elizabeth
Graphic design by Steven Durland

CONTENTS

ACKNOWLEDGEMENT

THE WORK OF THIS PROJECT, from conception and design, field interviews and analysis, to writing and publication has been an extensive collaboration between people from a wide range of background and experience, bonded by the extraordinary work of community artists and their partners. The way of this collaboration has been smoothed by a high degree of respect and openly honored interdependence among all participants. Perhaps this is due in part to the nature of the field, in which so much is accomplished through partnerships and mutual endeavor. However, the consistent good will and generosity of spirit practiced by everyone involved have graced this project in a fashion that feels uncommon and humbling. People, not institutions, make things happen. The successes of this project are the result of audience members who have shared their own time and hope for theater in their communities, university administrators who have been consistent and faithful in their support, colleagues who have applauded and challenged through every phase of the project, and the more than 50 community arts practitioners, artists and partners interviewed on site. With profound gratitude the project leadership thanks each and all. The following paragraphs outline a hint of the web this project represents.

Robert H. Leonard

EDITOR'S PREFACE

THIS BOOK IS ABOUT THE INFINITELY DIVERSE ways in which community is being built by a select group of artists across the country: eight theater ensembles (communities themselves) who have been working collaboratively in the places where they live for ten to 35 years.

These theaters are expressive of life in inner-city Los Angeles, small-town northern California, the African-American South, multicultural southern Texas, low-income central Appalachia, the economically struggling South Bronx of New York and cross-continental Native America.

The book is based on dozens of interviews with the artists themselves, their coworkers, their neighbors, their audiences and even their funders. The stories tell...

- How Cornerstone Theater Company is using peoples' stories to build bridges between communities of faith across the huge metropolis of L.A.

- How Carpetbag Theatre Company is working with the African-American community in Knoxville, Tennessee, to revise history and participate in a cultural revolution.

- How the Dell'Arte Company of Blue Lake, California, is creating a center for civic dialog around the rebirth of their tiny timber town into something new.

- How Jump-Start Performance Co. has risked its life to become a cultural intersection for the most diverse community in Texas, from Chicano traditions to gay performance art.

- How WagonBurner Theater Troop is placing creativity in the hands of its people so they can tell their own stories in

1

ancient communities scattered across Native America.

- How Los Angeles Poverty Department is making a safe space out of the most dangerous and transitory neighborhood in the city: Skid Row.

- How Roadside Theater and the people of central are truing the picture of a rural community exploited and lied about for 200 years.

- How Teatro Pregones is creating a place of welcome and comfort for the people of the Puerto Rican diaspora in the Bronx, New York.

As we go to press, ensemble theater is in the spotlight. A new national organization, the Network of Ensemble Theaters, is providing visibility for the field, and it sponsored the first U.S. national ensemble theater festival in 2005. The work has caught the attention of critics and grantmakers, who have created a body of new writing and funding programs around it. Graduate degree programs focusing on ensemble theater are beginning to appear, along with institutes offering multidisciplinary professional training collaborative methodology. A number of ensemble-theater leaders have been honored with national awards, such as the Ford Foundation's Leadership for a Changing World, the Heinz Award for Arts and Humanities and the MacArthur Fellowship or so-called "Genius" award.

These ensembles have been doing the bedrock work of building this country from its center, from its grass roots, and doing it in the most innovative and unexpected ways. It is lasting work because it is lighting the fires of creativity in the hearts of thousands of Americans of every description, who are carrying that fire to millions in their families, neighborhoods and workplaces.

I know that my own life would be far less rich and fulfilled without the work of these artists. They have changed me and the organizations I have founded. In ways that we have tried to preserve between these covers, they have changed the world. As time rushes on, I think we will all look back on the last 30 years as a Golden Age of art in the public interest.

Linda Frye Burnham, 2006

INTRODUCTION

The Ecology of Theater-in-community: A Field Theory
By Jan Cohen-Cruz

WENDELL BERRY UNDERSTANDS THE IDEA of culture by way of its etymological cousin, agriculture. The traditions, new ideas and interactions that generate systems of human meaning-making are like the particular soil, amount of rainfall and growing season that determine the particularities of plant life. Sandy soil is not better than loamy soil: the former gets you blueberries, the latter mushrooms. That genre of theater that stays close to its origins in terms of place, ethnicity or circumstances, sometimes known as grassroots or community-based, is the subject of this essay. These sources account for intimate interaction with audiences and can also contribute to the making of great theater. This model flies in the face of the conventional wisdom that art making is a self-contained process weakened by close community involvement.

This book is based on 1,000 pages of interviews with artists, staff, audiences and extended community members of eight theater ensembles: Carpetbag, Cornerstone, Dell'Arte, Jump-Start, LAPD (Los Angeles Poverty Department), Pregones, Roadside and WagonBurner. I'll introduce these companies by the characteristics that link them strongly enough to manifest a field, especially the primacy of place, deep interaction with constituents, and commitment to goals including and exceeding the creation of great theater. I'll also point out differences among them that confound the simple definition with which this field has been plagued. These theaters are part of a great tradition of art in community context, as I'll sketch out in a section on historical

3

sources. I'll describe the political ramifications of their various aesthetic approaches and the mechanisms by which they are grounded in their communities.

Characteristics of Grassroots Ensemble Theater

I have identified the linked characteristics of these theaters as: primacy of place, deep interaction with constituents and commitment to goals including and exceeding the creation of great theater. In fact, these characteristics are not just linked, they are inseparable from each other. Dedication to a place both engenders and arises from interaction with the people in that place. Deep interaction with the people both arises from and engenders need to make great theater and to go beyond that.

The social ecosystem I am describing situates these ensembles somewhere between theater and ritual. In grassroots theater, communities are involved with the art before, during, and after productions; as in ritual, they are necessary to the art's existence in ways well beyond economic support. Unlike mainstream professional shows, a grassroots theater production in New Haven could not as likely have been created in Minneapolis or Washington, D.C. Whereas many of the same actors, directors and designers work at various mainstream theaters, you can't move all the local people who contribute in some way to grassroots productions. The word audience does not convey the pervasiveness of spectatorial interaction in grassroots theater. As scholar Richard Schechner said of ritual: "There is no audience participation in primeval or contemporary shamanistic performances because there is no audience. Rather there are circles of increasing intensity" (Schechner 1973: 243). Ritual performances (whether sacred as a church service or secular as a political inauguration) need the community because they assert "the group's shared and unquestionable truths" (Myerhoff 1978: 32). On the other hand, theater is open, contingent; a choice, not an obligation; an experiment, an "imagine if." The theaters in this field are on a continuum, not totally theater or ritual, any given production manifesting some measure of each.

Ritual is associated with efficacy, getting something done. Theater is associated with entertainment, often interpreted as the obligation to not get anything done but rather to exist for its own sake. Let both theater projects exist! Like those blueberries and mushrooms, different forms of cultural expression contribute different and valuable nutrients and flavors. Then too, it's not always obvious where efficacy or entertainment may take place. "Efficacy" is part of an ecosystem; a production is transformed by contemporary circumstances. One of my most efficacious experiences at the theater was at a Broadway production of "Falsettos" in 1992. As the characters mourned the loss of Whizzer to AIDS, I wept at the loss of my dear pal David, and inadvertently leaned in to the stranger to my left. He, weeping with an abandon that also seemed to transcend the death of the character, leaned in to me, communicating great empathy. Everywhere I saw weeping spectators, and felt that the theatrical event had transformed into a mass public funeral for our beloveds lost to AIDS.

Grassroots theater is about not just the play but the play in its community context. I experienced this profoundly in 1969, having just landed my first job as a professional actress with the Players' Theater of Manchester, New Hampshire. Thanks to a Title I grant, through which the federal government matched local funds, we were performing in little towns dotted all across the White Mountains. People in one particular town wanted to book our play, based on New Hampshire favorite son Daniel Webster, but wouldn't know how much money they could contribute until the night of the performance, intending to raise it by holding a potluck supper just before the show. But they could promise us a delicious dinner. We accepted these terms, and arrived at the town hall amidst great excitement. Nearly every spectator was also a producer of a scrumptious dish, setting up a sense of reciprocity such as I had seldom experienced at any event. The spirit of exchange infused the performance itself, accounting for extra generosity on the actors' part and extra receptivity from the spectators. Simply, we were part of an all-too-rare relationship of equal exchange. This "communitas," or

community leveling and bonding as facilitated by the performance process, is another link between grassroots and ritual performance. (See the work of anthropologist Victor Turner for
more on communitas.)

In contrast, mainstream theater as an institution carries a
whole apparatus of hierarchy. Those able to leverage the most
money are on top, be they producers or stars. The playwright is
generally second, demonstrating western civilization's bias for
written expression over the oral and physical. Next comes the
director, then the rest of the "creative team" designers, com-
posers, and choreographers. Then the actors, mere interpreters,
followed by the even more lowly technicians, mere "skilled
workers." Last and least, if discussed at all, is the audience. A
few years after my New Hampshire experience, performing in an
"out-of-town" (read New York for "town") try-out house, I had
the horrible sensation that there was no one in the audience. It
wasn't the bright lights on stage and the auditorium in darkness
a community-based play may choose such a lighting design to
support focus. Conceived as an out-of-town try-out, the performance was less for the actual spectators there than as a preparation for elsewhere. In a profound way the audience we were
performing for was not there.

Community-based ensembles strive for a more egalitarian ideal.
They do not embrace the star system. Everyone has some creative
in-put. Carpetbag Theatre member Linda Hill describes this as
"community-theater-cause-I-want-a-place-to-have-an-artistic-
voice model." Playwrights literally "wright" i.e., hammer out
plays, often from materials gathered locally. Acclaimed choreographers like Liz Lerman and Jawole Willa Jo Zollar have created
techniques to incorporate movement from everyone's gestures.
This collective creativity reflects the purposes of the ensembles
that include but go beyond art making, and are evident from the
very moment of their founding. In 1969, local activists, artists,
and educators note that they were not only theater makers founded Carpetbag, "rooted in the desire to have a voice that is uniquely from this community." Cornerstone began when a group of
Harvard graduates, led by Bill Rauch and Alison Carey, rejected

the model of regional theaters whose audiences are presumed to be homogenous, and set off for small towns and urban neighborhoods to reach a diversity more representative of the country's regions and peoples. Jump-Start's artistic director Steve Bailey says, "It's about making an exchange with a community, which doesn't solely happen via the theater work."

Place is significant to all grassroots theaters. Roadside Theater of Appalachia is "made from the history and cultural traditions of this place, by ensemble members who grew up and remain in this place." Banjos and ballads accompany wily working-class heroes in traditional stories. Roadside is currently developing a play based on songs and history bespeaking the 200-year history of Scotch-Irish settlers in the region, from core actor-musician-writer Ron Short's research into his own family. Yet innovation is also omnipresent. Stories are adapted to contemporary circumstances and traditional aesthetics are influenced by partnerships with artists rooted in other sources. Short's major collaborator in the current project is Beegie Adair, a jazz pianist and recording artist based in Nashville.

The Dell'Arte Company in northern California also advocate a philosophy of theater of place "created by, for and about the area in which you live. Artists can earn community support while challenging parochialism, bigotry, insularity, apathy; they balance experimentation with awareness of what the audience wants, likes, hopes for, can tolerate, will be inspired by." Founder Carlo Mazzone-Clementi brought a physical theater aesthetic based in European popular theater with him when he settled in Blue Lake in 1974. That "outsider" technique is grounded with "insider" content: "local characters and issues are frequently the subject of original stories that reveal voices and points of view that can be absorbed by the community from a new perspective."

The movement's commitment to particular communities is exemplified by Carpetbag Theatre of Knoxville, which serves a broad local constituency "based upon a shared sense of place, particular traditions or their desire for a just world." A commitment to homeless people is core for LAPD, founded in 1985. LAPD's performance style reflects the energy of its Skid Row neighborhood and depends on improvisation. The ensemble confounds the notion that theater with nonprofessionals is only about constituents' lives and for therapeutic purposes: LAPD plays are a wild, stream-of-consciousness mix of fact, fiction and fantasy. Such theater relies on a high level of skill on the directors' part; director John Malpede finds creative ways to deal with performance mishaps inevitable with untrained people. For example, cast members not in a given scene often remain on stage, ready to call out lines as needed.

When a theater is ethnically homogeneous, sense of place can be more complex. Sometimes it is a sense of many places or a sense of loss of place. WagonBurner director LeAnne Howe says, "The U.S. is our community, from which we draw American Indian actors." WB began in 1993 in Iowa City, with university students, faculty, and friends. "In the middle of the country, the pinnacle of non-diversity, conservatism in that lack of community we created our own, which is why I think we consider ourselves a community theater." They took the things they needed to say "almost like a holy mission," and educated Iowans. Inactive for several years, the ensemble is centered around special events that teach the history of native people. They are also committed to dialog between under- and misrepresented groups, such as Native and African-Americans. The mission of Teatro Pregones in the Bronx, New York, attests to their commitment to both ethnic grounding and multicultural exchange: "to create innovative, challenging theater rooted in Puerto Rican traditions and popular artistic expressions, and to present performing artists from different cultures, offering Latinos and other communities an artistic means to affirm and enhance our roles in society." Researcher Arnaldo López reflects that Pregones' 22-year trajectory as a Puerto Rican arts organization has meant addressing questions of "self-determination, identity, displacement, continuity and belonging." Pregones is translocal, which "describes the unfixed geography of Latinos in the US." Eighty-five percent of their audiences are Latinos who often travel from some distance to see them.

Building bridges between and within diverse communities is stated in Cornerstone's mission. Initially doing so in towns all across the U.S., they have since settled in Los Angeles. Scholar Sonja Kuftinec identifies a core goal of Cornerstone and community-based theater generally as "creating collectively generated theater with non-professionals" (Kuftinec:10). The more local people engage with the work, the greater their emotional and intellectual investment, which in turn sharpens a production's aim and its potential for impact. Cornerstone helps a community find a story it most needs to tell, then facilitates that telling. In what they call bridge shows, three or more communities enter a single collaboration. Professionals and community residents conduct research, gather materials in workshop and focus groups, develop and stage a play that is "by, for, and about the community." Jump-Start Performance Co. in San Antonio also emphasizes cultural diversity; their mission is "innovation in performance form or content; to be a lasting voice of diverse cultures & address critical issues of our times." JS members resist definition, staying open to more and more people and groups. They are committed to a "diversity of under-heard voices. Involvement in the community fuels the fire, inspires the work."

These eight companies are diverse geographically, both urban and rural, and grounded in different places, cultures and traditions. Most of these ensembles maintain a company of artists who also create their own unique work and co-define the company's mission. They share commitments to active cultural and civic participation, partnering with local institutions like schools, housing works, social-justice organizations, universities and occasionally regional theaters, thus manifesting the spirit of participatory democracy. Recalling her work in the 1970s with The Road Company (an ensemble directed by this study's co-investigator Bob Leonard), Kathie deNobriga writes that it was "located in the unlikely town of Johnson City, Tennessee. I knew it was unlikely because it was only 20 miles away from the town I grew up in. Having absorbed some of the 'You're so good, why aren't you in New York?' mentality, I consider it one of my life's ambitions to make sure every young person makes that same discovery: that heightened sense of self-worth, sense of place, of community, of making a difference as a person and an artist" (1993: 11).

The Great Tradition of Art in Community Contexts

Linda Frye Burnham estimates that there are "more than 50, but fewer than 100" professional grassroots theaters across the U.S. The field interweaves an assortment of historical threads. The tapestry extends far and wide. One thread is the art/life movement, which theoretically encompasses experimental art practices such as John Cage's expansion of music to any sound, as well as amateur art overflowing aesthetic boundaries at church suppers, 4th of July patriotic pageants and other civic occasions. Open to everyone, at broadly accessible sites and around themes of everyday interest, bringing art and life close together is a recurrent response of 20th century artists for whom theater is overly elite. LAPD's John Malpede might be seen in this tradition. Malpede was a performance artist who arrived in Los Angeles as homeless people were being removed from the streets in preparation for the 1986 Olympics. He quickly began a theater workshop on Skid Row which he has continued via LAPD ever since. "The power of this group's work," avows Malpede, "is a burr under the saddle of those who would segregate community art from High Art."

Another thread is activist performances such as have accompanied the struggles of workers (e.g., the Paterson Strike Pageant of 1913), people of color (as, DuBois' Krigwa Players), and women (such as suffragette theatrics) throughout the 20th century. This reached a critical mass in the late 1960s/ early 70s, when a handful of aesthetically exciting and socially engaged ensembles served as cultural wings of political movements the San Francisco Mime Troupe re: free speech, the Free Southern Theater re: the Civil Rights Movement, El Teatro Campesino vis-à-vis the United Farm Workers and Bread & Puppet re: the anti-(Vietnam) war movement. Exemplary in this regard is Carpetbag Theatre, begun in 1969 as part of the cultural expression of Black Power responding to a national call for arts programming relevant and useful to black experience. Linda Parris-Bailey, artistic director, explains: "Things we were reading about, like the Free Southern Theater, were shaping how I was interpreting and moving forward as a theater artist. My whole notion was what could happen through theater tied to activism. There was that mood, that support, that education about what was going on in the country. I came to Carpetbag in 1974 with all those notions." Nayo Watkins, who conducted the Carpetbag research for "Performing Communities," became a writer and an activist during the Civil Rights Movement. Like others who came of age in that context, what she learned about art making and social justice then has animated her work in communities ever since (2000). Artistic Director Dudley Cocke attributes the Civil Rights Movement as a catalyst to Roadside, too.

The great social movements stretching from the 1950s and the push for civil rights shifted in strategy from popular activism to advocacy and professionalized efforts. By the late 1970s, a localized impulse manifested itself as identity politics, with artists, too, clustering around communities of ethnicity (as, Latino), circumstances (as, elderly) and orientation (as, gay). Dell'Arte supporter Peter Pennekamp identifies this as a move from opposition to affirmation, citing Bernice Johnson Reagon's insight: "Remember when you first recognized injustice? And thought that if you saw it you could change it? Joined with like-minded people, worked at it for years, and eventually felt somewhat defeated? You know what was wrong with the way we approached it? We went out to do battle every day to win, rather than because it was the right way to lead a life." The result is what Lucy Lippard calls "the lure of the local," less about fighting injustice generally than providing alternative voices on the local level. Equally appealing to some grassrooters like Dell'Arte's Joan Schirle was the opportunity to make a life in the country and still pursue a rigorous physically based acting style.

Woven amidst all these threads is an emphasis on participation and access, evidenced in the early 20th century pageant movement. Whether motivated by a conservative impulse to quickly absorb new immigrants or by progressive attempts to get women the vote, groups of people with a shared core identity performed tableaux and spectacles in public spaces, often for thousands of spectators. The Little Theater Movement decentralized performing arts beyond the big cities, laying the groundwork for both the professional regional theater and community-based movements of the past 40 years. From 1919 until the Great Depression, the Harlem Renaissance demonstrated a great range of creativity on the part of African Americans. Workers theater in the 1920s and 1930s engaged thousands of people not hitherto part of the U.S. theater scene, though many immigrants had been artistically inclined in "the old country." The Federal Theater Project (1935-1939) was a massive, gloriously eclectic government-supported effort to put theater professionals back to work all across the U.S. Although Alexander Drummond was already at work at Cornell in the 1920s, universities picked up some of post-Federal Theater Project slack, with Frederick Koch in North Carolina and others developing what Robert Gard practiced in Wisconsin and wrote about in "Grassroots Theater" (1955), "plays that grow from all the countrysides of America."

As much about place as Roadside Theater is, Cocke was not familiar with Gard when he co-founded Roadside in 1975-6. But he embraced the term grassroots which came to identify the movement over the past 20 years. Cocke, Harry Newman and Janet Salmons-Rue theorized it as:

> A theater that comes from and serves those with the least power in the society. Over the decades this kind of theater has been described by various names and is now commonly referred to as "community-based." [It is connected] to progressive political work which similarly gets its support and draws its inspiration from the bottom instead of the top, from the broadest range of people. The defining characteristic of grassroots theater is to preserve and express the values of those without privilege (1993: 13).

Burnham identifies grassroots as one of two flanks in community-based art, the other emerging from the avant-garde. She writes,

> While many artists were dropping out of the mainstream in the '60s, the great wave came in about 1970 when the

Boomer generation got out of grad school and began dropping out because they were resistant to the market atmosphere surrounding it. This not only took the artists out of the art palaces and into the streets, it created a revolution in art forms. Some artists rooted themselves in conceptual art, work that couldn't be sold. Performance art was born from this seed (2002).

Several other historical markers are important to note. Bob Leonard emphasizes the Living Theater, founded in 1951, which worked in a community of alternative-minded people and aspired to art integrated in life (hence its name). He suggests a progression from the short-lived period during which artists disenchanted with the status quo dropped out, then sought alternative communities, and then connected with community partners. CETA grants, in the late 1970s, provided artists with economic support; equally important, many required artists to have community partners. As Leonard points out, "Sometimes arranged marriages work." Alternate ROOTS (Regional Organization of Theaters South), founded in 1976, is also part of this history, as well as an important membership organization in the present (though some longtime members feel that it has lost focus). Ruby Lerner, a former director of ROOTS, sees this movement as "the contemporary manifestation of a recurring cultural ideal of an art relegated not to culture palaces, but relevant to daily life, an art whose home is in the streets, in schools, church basements, city parks, and other institutions dear to community life" (1994: 15). While performances in alternative sites are not categorically preferred, a Teatro Pregones member points out that being housed in a church for many years kept as many people away as it welcomed, the spirit of Lerner's remarks would likely be embraced by all the ensembles examined here.

The Ecology of Grassroots Aesthetics and Politics

One of the debates concerning grassroots theater is the question of radicality. The movement is radical in the American Heritage

Dictionary sense of "arising from or going to a root or source." The source consists of a broad base of people from whom cultural traditions emanate but who are typically left out of art and policy-making activities. While grassroots theaters may not advocate change per se, their commitment to audiences of every class and race is contrary to mainstream theater audience composition of the wealthiest 15% of the population. Burnham believes that grassroots is often equated with left-wing politics because of the term's association with organizing, "meaning you can't accomplish change without going to the roots of the problem and including the people whose feet are planted in that place, maybe even being those people."

Both grassroots and community-based imply that theater is not a self-contained entity but rather gains meaning in a context, integrated in people's lives. But community-based artists do not necessarily share a core identity with the people in the contexts in which they work. They can catalyze and support but are less likely to sustain radicality because they constantly move on to other projects. Grassroots theater practitioners sometimes begin as outsiders e.g., Dell'Arte members moving to Blue Lake but become insiders, sharing their constituents' way of life, essaying to eliminate boundaries. When Cornerstone Theater traveled from town to town they made community-based plays with local residents; settled now in Los Angeles, they are becoming a grassroots company, albeit stretching the term by all the ways that they define connectedness.

Floating the idea of grassroots theater as the left flank of the community-based realm brought this response from Bob Leonard:

> I agree that "grassroots" carries within it the implication of a radical, rather than a liberal agenda, which is I think most appropriate for these eight. However, I feel uneasy with the language of "left wing," which is inevitably tinged with the communist/socialist paradigm of another era. I think radical in our times, as these companies' choices bear out, is about finding new agendas, new strategies, and new takes on popular democratic action.

I appreciate Leonard's call for a paradigm for our times, and can understand a hesitancy to enter a community with what may seem like outsider political language. Yet many of these groups demonstrate the ongoing relevance of lessons learned from art expressive of left wing ideals. Bertolt Brecht, who sometimes referred to his oeuvre as dialectic theater, may be seen as a direct forbear of the contemporary progressive movement for art-based civic dialog. Augusto Boal, an avid Workers' Party activist, and his "theatre of the oppressed" is an inspiration to many of the companies in this project. Leonard's distinction between "popular democratic" and "left wing" sometimes blurs; both stand for access to and participation by all.

Linda Burnham's response to grassroots as community-based's left flank was as follows:

> I think it would sharpen our writing and perspective and make for some interesting analysis: To what degree are these people focused on change? We need to make pretty sure that is how these theaters see themselves. I know plenty of artists who walk way around that term, because they don't want to ever go into a community with an overt agenda of change; it's a little imperialistic. I wonder how Blue Lake would feel if they suddenly discovered they were harboring artists whose reason for being there was to change it. In that sense, I don't think Dell'Arte is radical, and that's the difference between them and the S.F. Mime Troupe. Their agenda now is pretty much to open questions for discussion, not accomplish change in the sense that John O'Neal is [i.e., Junebug Productions' artistic director O'Neal, committed to art that improves the lot of poor, working-class and oppressed people].

These responses confirm a tension between the two senses of radicality, i.e., rooted in community and left-wing. They converge in a shared principle: "arise from or go to a root or source" rather than to impose from on high, i.e., facilitate the self-expression of communities that have a vested interest in change from the status quo. Paradoxically, such companies are often conservative in the sense of preserving or celebrating a cultural heritage. Another challenge to the embrace of radicality is that such ensembles will only survive if they can sell some of their productions. Dell'Arte's marketing director, Dave Firney, told me that they had to take some of their more radical (as in challenging the status quo) productions out of circulation because they could not book them.

Problematic for the field, the terms "grassroots" and "community-based" often evoke inaccurate images. According to Pregones, both labels signify "lacking in rigor," causing mainstream audiences to withdraw. Malpede rebels against "community-based" as a code word for "bad" theater and the assumption that it is primarily therapeutic for participants, flatly reflective of their lives, and of no aesthetic value. Cocke finds "community-based" too vague: all theater comes from some community. Others see "grassroots" as too integrally allied with the idea of social change, which is not always the work's goal. These are professional ensembles, and if "grassroots" connotes an activity done by amateurs alone, it is undermining. Long-time cultural theorists Don Adams and Arlene Goldbard now prefer the term "community cultural development," which they define as "a range of initiatives undertaken by artists in collaboration with other community members to express identity, concerns and aspirations through the arts and communication media, while building cultural capacity and contributing to social change" (2001:107). I find "development" too redolent of "underdeveloped countries," and I miss an aesthetic marker (the word art or theater). Do any of these terms: theater "of common ground," "of exchange," or Dudley·Cocke's suggestion, "theater of inclusion," capture the spirit of the field with fewer drawbacks?

Although grassroots theaters get flack from some for being too radical and others for not being radical enough, at their best they shape responses to any concerns of their constituencies. Pennekamp points out how knowing the community merges the political with the psycho-social; for example, Dell'Arte "articulated that the issue of timber decline wasn't just jobs, but a whole notion of being taken care of by an industry. This was the first time that had been raised." Grassroots theaters invite collective input vis-à-vis choice of project themes, script development, ownership and responsibility. Most do some productions in collaboration with community participants. This is as much an aesthetic as a political choice. Says Cornerstone's Bill Rauch, "There's something aesthetic about the variety of ages and body types and life experience, a diversity that is part of the fabric of the work, and that's what makes it powerful." Cornerstone and most others do some productions with just the core company because, says Rauch, "there are certain muscles that we can only exercise with ensemble members."

Many of these ensembles situate themselves within culturally syntonic traditions that bring depth to both their craft and to their relationship with particular audiences and communities. For example, Roadside's immersion in Appalachian music and storytelling engages a broad local audience at productions at home in Whitesburg, Kentucky, just as Pregones' intimate knowledge of Puerto Rican theater and music packs Latino audiences (and others) into their performances in the Bronx. Innovation is equally core; as artists they allow themselves the freedom to experiment and reinterpret traditions for their particular time and place. As Roadside's Dudley Cocke explains, "People who work with a consciousness of a tradition, whatever it is, have even more incentive to be creative than artists who are unconscious of tradition. They know what's already been invented which is the springboard for inventing something else. Otherwise you're flailing around with no sense of where you're going because you have no sense of where it's been" (2002).

Beyond these common practices, aesthetics vary widely. The signature grassroots approach is personal story-based, which offers people a subjective way to respond to social circumstances. Roadside members introduced story circles to Appalachia to bring back storytelling traditions there. The company's aesthetic is equally musical theater: Cocke explains, "Our native ballad tradition, by definition, is story-based" (2002). From the Appalachian region themselves, ensemble members grew up surrounded by these traditions. One of their joint artistic/political goals is to break stereotypes about Appalachians, an expression of commitment to the people of that place. Story circles are also core on tour; Cocke defines the goal of Roadside's residencies as "to help a community listen to itself, learn about itself, and express itself publicly so that participants can hear and appreciate their own words" (2000). He also attests to the historically political role of stories as "dissenting oral narratives arising from suppressed histories" (2002).

Dell'Arte and Pregones are grounded in different yet also non-literary approaches: a great range of European and Latino popular theater traditions, respectively. Popular theater has historically relied on techniques accessible to people no matter what their education, such as the physical, archetypal Italian commedia dell'arte and Mexican carpa, or tent show. The popular is often linked with democratization of theater, extending to the working class by virtue of content, form and venue. The French tradition of the popular was articulated by Romain Rolland in his book, "Le theater du peuple" (1903), described by theater historian Marvin Carlson as "a theater accessible to the workers without being condescending, and educative without being pompous or exclusive. He proposed for it three basic concerns: to provide relaxation for its patrons after a day of labor, to give them energy for the day to come, and to stimulate their minds" (1993:317).

The popular also bespeaks a sense of broad cultural ownership. Pregones member Jorge Merced describes a performance at a high school that began really badly but when the Latino music and poetry started, the whole event turned around. Pregones acknowledges the influence of Boal (Brazilian), Buenaventura (Colombian), Osvaldo Dragún (Argentinean), and collective/political/experimental Latin American Teatro Popular and Nuevo Teatro. These sources share popular theater's emphasis on theater as a communal event, participating in the celebratory, political and effective life of the populace.

Many grassroots ensembles work in contemporary genres. LAPD reflects Malpede's grounding in experimental, stream-of-consciousness techniques. That LAPD artists have not attended The Academy is the point: Malpede believes that artists encounter and express forces and situations that the rest of us are unwilling or unable to. Malpede asserts, "LAPD artists send back messages as vital in this regard as any other artist." Carpetbag called a recent piece a hip-hop opera. Jump-Start favors original interdisciplinary work. Company members' proposals are usually accepted but initiators must carry the work load that comes with it and share a vision of a changing world and disenfranchised voices. Jump-Start considers its ideas of inclusion at once reflective of participatory democracy and an aesthetics of taking risks. Cornerstone is most known for adapting classical plays via intensive community interviewing though they sometimes create plays from scratch with a playwright, company and local participants. Rauch explains, "The company's aesthetic is to include the community's dialog with itself in the script, which calls for opposing voices and layers of meaning and a vital richness. Multiplicity of viewpoints: it's essential to our mission."

WagonBurner creates a close rapport with audiences by breaking the fourth wall "it's not TV" and encouraging participation. The ensemble looks for humor without offending: "Don't enjoy yourself as an actor at a character's expense." For example, director Howe felt that one actor's characterization "told more about how a straight male thinks about a gay male than how the gay male might interact in the situation." Their plays' "Indian-style" humor is intended to educate, break stereotypes, keep you from just being depressed. White audiences are often afraid of offending them, and don't laugh till the actors give permission. The name "WagonBurner" captures the satire and anger "Yeah, we're Indians, those savages who fried your ancestors; where were they going and on whose land by the way?"

Community-based theaters manifest a deep belief in the power of art to bring different people together, and the result is that stereotypes are cracked open in the unfolding of the art. Seeing Roadside's bluegrass gospel singers and pickers perform with an African-American gospel quartet reinforces similarities among people such as integrating song into everyday life and the centrality of spiritual expression as well as nonhierarchical, aesthetically pleasing differences in harmonies, styles and instrumentation. Blueberries and mushrooms.

Mechanisms Grounding Ensembles in Their Communities

Community-based theaters can be deeply integrated with their constituencies because theater is not just the performance but all the processes leading up to and following after it. Schechner articulated the phases of performance as training, workshop, rehearsal, warm-up, performance, cool-down and aftermath (1990). In what follows I suggest how these phases provide opportunities for deep exchange with communities. As concerns training, given this field's interdisciplinary nature, grounding in multiple skills in addition to the artistic is necessary. Dudley Cocke, for example, emphasizes the need for grassroots artists to learn community organizing. Alice Lovelace believes artists working for social change need training in conflict resolution. One must also be mindful of the attitudes particular techniques transmit to an audience. Interviewer Mark McKenna reflected about Dell'Arte's school: "Students come to understand the performer's responsibility to the audience." Commedia, for example, is an inherently interactive mode. The school's focus is also on creating one's own work, typical of this field as a whole, so it's about everyone's voice at that level, too. Steve Buescher, associate school director, says that before he did workshops with Michael Fields, he "didn't know that as an actor you could have your own thoughts."

The next phase, workshop, frequently incorporates communal input. Each Cornerstone community show involves an average of 20 meetings with local focus groups and leaders. The company begins by finding one local person "making the leap of faith" and becoming an advocate for the project, helping find appropriate people for an advisory board. Cornerstone tells the board how they build a project and the board advises the company how to do so there. In the development of the art work, integration of local stories is one way that different points of view are put into conversation with each other. Dell'Arte audience member Kit

Zettler emphasizes the cross-pollination this accomplishes: "You are not necessarily going to get a logger who comes see this play and walks away saying I'm never doing that again. But a logger comes to the play because their friend got interviewed or was talked to." He thus ends up hearing other points of view. In other projects, the community has a united point of view and creates the play as a form of advocacy. Both of these dynamics also take place during grassroots rehearsal processes.

Warm-up is the process immediately preceding a show. In plays meant to maximize audience participation, spectators are often given a way to prepare, too, perhaps through pre-performance interaction or actual warm-up exercises. Next, the performance itself offers various dynamic ways for actor-spectator exchange. Carpetbag's "Red Summer" was based on historical documentation of activist Knoxvillians during the civil-rights era. Director Linda Parris-Bailey saw it as a way to tell residents that their belief nothing could change was historically incorrect: "Maybe if we just remind you of what has been here before, you can see some possibility for the future. We talk about people who take control." Parris-Bailey sees a fundamentally celebratory component in the company's historical pieces. Pregones' "The Embrace" is an example of a production using Boal's forum theater to engage audience dialog on the spot. Forum invites spectators to replace a protagonist struggling with a social issue, in this case as a result of having AIDS. Spectators enact different possible ways of handling those struggles.

What Schechner calls the cool-down phase immediately follows performance and may take the form of discussion. Though often very effective, there's some ambivalence about this format. Sometimes spectators aren't ready to talk about a play so soon; sometimes artists bring in discussion leaders but audiences really only want to hear from artists. Pregones usually only uses dialog after a new show that they're trying to figure out; the conversation function as an evaluation. Sometimes panel experts learn as much as anyone else, as with LAPD's "Agents and Assets." Experts on developing countries and the CIA reported being educated by their outspoken and eloquent LAPD co-panelists from

Skid Row. In another example, Cornerstone, in a collaboration with Touchstone Theater, arranged post-show gatherings over dessert and drinks so spectators had unmediated conversation with each other. The artists of Alternate ROOTS often use critical response from the audience after showing a work in progress. This has led to the development of Liz Lerman's Critical Response Process, which puts the artist herself in charge of the feedback session.

Aftermath/long-term activities not immediately following the artwork take the initiative further. For example, during the years that Cornerstone did residencies in towns across the U.S., they regularly donated money for each community to start a theater. LAPD partners with SRO Housing, which has renovated 30 former slum hotels into "single-room occupancy" hotels. They share the overall mission of helping people off the street, to build a life. LAPD adds a creative dimension to SRO which in turn lends an infrastructure that nurtures LAPD. Many interviewees said that seeing one of the eight ensembles influenced a later decision to become actively involved in political/civic life. Like Susan Ingalls' concept of "the key positive experience," it's often not till years later that people realize they had a transformative experience through art (Cohen-Cruz and Novak, 1998).

Still and all, the relationship with the community ought not be romanticized. Sometimes the artists are more ready for change than is the community; Parris-Bailey describes the need for sensitivity given that her community is not so proactive: "The community is sometimes challenged and needs to be challenged, and sometimes they don't like that. But that's a part of how we all grow. So it's not that we have to constantly please." Roadside describes a need to "begin where the community participants are. Not ahead (unrealistic) or behind (patronizing)." Every ensemble in the study attests to the lack of what Jump-Start's Steve Bailey expresses as "enough time, money and staff to do the creation of new work and community projects both well." Because many of the companies are run by the artists themselves, they also have heavy administrative loads.

Not to be underestimated is the ongoing struggle on many theaters' part for fuller communal engagement. Dell'Arte's July 2002 project is a case in point. "Wild Card" is a piece about the opening of a casino on Native American land in Blue Lake amidst a great range of communal responses. The ensemble was not able to engage people of different opinions, especially Native Americans, as fully in the making of the piece as they had hoped. Thanks to an Animating Democracy Initiative grant, a dialog specialist sat down with six Native Americans and heard their points of view. But Artistic Director Michael Fields expressed some frustration at the difficulty of having such exchange more regularly.

Another challenge is apparent in the past tense of grounding: grounded. While on the one hand grounded refers to a deep-seated sense of self, there is also the colloquial meaning of being forced to stay home. Some ensembles risk becoming overly insulated. Jump-Start members express their need and that of their community for exposure to the rest of the world, to see what artists elsewhere are doing and what they can add to it. They regularly present artists from elsewhere. Dell'Arte, too, bridges its geographic isolation by connecting with other cultures, artists and trends: "We bring you things from around the world and down the block." Pregones, Roadside and Cornerstone likewise have formidable touring schedules that bring in both money and contact with other audiences and artists. Malpede has done projects with the homeless in cities all across the U.S.

Most of the ensembles express concerns related to sustainability. Would they continue after the founder or artistic director was no longer with them? If so, how? Core members frequently work for little pay, 24/7. Seldom will someone hired on later accept such conditions. Many ensembles have tried to bring in younger artists but none seem totally secure that the next generation will take up the organizational reins. On the other hand, a delicate situation arises when longtime company members are not producing up to par. These ensembles are never just professional; people give their blood and soul, so it's very hard to fire them down the line. How can ensembles be responsible to people without whom they may not have ever existed and still use limited monies at the service of the company's greatest needs? One of the ensembles was trying to solve this by restructuring core artists' duties, but there are no definitive answers.

Then there's passing on the aesthetic approach. Dell'Arte already has a school and Cornerstone is developing one. Some techniques of popular theater are taught in professional programs in universities or elsewhere; CAN (the Community Arts Network, the source of this project) publishes an online list of such opportunities. Members of some companies express anti-university sentiments. Pregones' Jorge Merced described it as a "less committed approach, less sense of being given the role to make your own." To me, it's a question of what kind of university training; though even great university training is too expensive. Others have had very productive university-based collaborations, such as Roadside's three-year residency at Cornell in the mid '90s. Carpetbag has a relationship with Knoxville College; WagonBurner began at Iowa State.

A healthy relationship with academic institutions is just one ingredient of a well-established field. Others include a discourse both orally via conferences and in print via books, journals and Websites; membership organizations where practitioners can meet, share, question, develop; places to train the next generation; agreed-upon categories of assessment; and sustainable sources of money. But first funders need to know what their grant money is going for. They need to understand the field as a contemporary expression of a very old theatrical paradigm: art that expresses, generates and challenges meaning in a specific community. Rather than conceived as old-fashioned ("Let's put on a play!") and amateurish, these theaters embrace an ecological expression of art as a balance between conceptualizers and receivers, rather than a hot-house flower on display. Those of us who have worked on *Performing Communities* hope that our effort will help towards the sustenance of this field.

FINDINGS: Knowing the Secrets Behind the Laughter
By Robert H. Leonard and Ann Kilkelly

Last year's play for the festival, there was a lot of political stuff in town going on. They incorporated that into the play, and if you weren't from town it was funny. But if you were from town, you really had belly laughs because you knew the secrets behind it.

Gene Supka
Proprietor, The Logger Bar
Blue Lake, California

THE IMPULSE TO FIND OUT MORE about successful ensemble work deeply rooted in communities has driven this project from its start. We looked at eight theater ensembles working in various regions of the United States with the intention to identify the specific qualities that mark each of them as highly discrete, individualized artistic efforts and to identify shared knowledge, perceptions and practices that might lead to a deeper understanding of a vision common to them all. We selected these particular eight ensembles for their diversity of size, longevity, location and artistic focus.

Our inquiry was framed by three questions:

1. What does theater rooted in community (or grassroots theater) mean to the participants? [The term "participants" includes everyone involved in the theater experience from conception through performance and subsequent community events.]

2. What tangible and intangible results happen in the community as a result of the group's work? And, vice versa, what are the

effects of the community on the group and its work?

3. What do the participants describe as successful practices?

The practical design of the project incorporated in-depth site visits. On the principle, established in the work of *High Performance* magazine, that artists are themselves resources for constructive observation and critical dialog, the site visitors selected by the project were artists with deep personal experience in grassroots ensemble theater. Site visitors spent at least three days, and in some cases considerably more, with the ensembles, attending performances and events, collecting inventories of documentary resources, taking in as much of the group's culture and environment as possible, and conducting interviews. They interviewed not only the artists in the eight ensembles, but also staff, board, audience and community members, funders and scholars in community art.

The investigators approached this project on the premise that the many participants in an artistic enterprise – the artist, the audience, the community sources and partners – are essential voices in the development and understanding of the theories and practices of community art making.

Listening to these voices and contemplating the field notes of the site visitors, we discovered that it is productive to look at this work in three ways:

- describing theoretical approaches
- identifying specific practices
- recognizing the results of the work of these ensembles

Theoretical Approaches

The most important thing we learned in studying these eight ensembles is that they are all singularly committed to creating plays for live performance that originate out of the community in which the artists work. Each of these ensembles makes work in, from and for specific communities. In fact, the community is itself a primary ingredient to the creative process in wonderful and surprising ways that differ ensemble by ensemble and project by project.

However, it is first crucial to recognize that when theater is made in such intimate collaboration between artists and community, the histories, cultures, traditions, cares, concerns, questions, faiths, doubts, fears, perspectives and experiences of the community are more than present, they are essential to the plays made. The plays of these ensembles are expressions of the communities from which they emerge. They are, therefore, essentially political, that is, of the polis or town. These ensembles, their audiences and their community partners understand the intimate and sophisticated relationship of community and its art. Sometimes the plays speak what everybody knows; sometimes they speak what nobody says. Sometimes they open paths or unveil truths; sometimes they challenge the way things are done or understood. Sometimes the storyteller slays the dragon; sometimes the storyteller is the dragon (to borrow from Jo Carson, a daring storyteller and well known community-based artist). The deeply political and social nature of these ensembles creates a realm of remarkable possibility and artistic wealth. It is the realm of theater every bit as much as it is the mysterious domain of the human soul. The artistic impulse to present the political and social infuses the aesthetics and the creative methods of these ensembles.

Yet, understanding how the aesthetic process is itself political requires a careful look at the assumptions often made about art with a clear social agenda. The term "political theater" carries with it certain unfortunate and misleading baggage – a cause-and-effect expectation for direct change: Do this to get a new set of street lights, to get a new government or a new way of life. The interviews of this study identify this baggage as entirely off the mark of their own realities and immaterial to their successes and challenges. To consider, to evaluate the work of these ensembles in terms of quantitative impact on social change is to miss the point entirely. These ensembles make art to be enjoyed and evaluated for what it reveals, how it engages and what it stimulates in the imaginations and lives of the participants. The politic of these ensembles is to make good art that is responsible to its community and is part of civic life. From this viewpoint, it is often a failure of civic life that it does not include work of the imagination in its emphases. Several ensemble members offer their own unique perspectives on this crucial matter.

Alison Carey, ensemble member of Cornerstone Theater Company, says bluntly, "Our primary job is to create good plays." She goes on, "Our art doesn't exist without the way our art is created, with the involvement of the community; and the involvement of the community wouldn't work with bad art." Joan Schirle goes into the substance of what she understands as good art when she describes how The Dell'Arte Company approached the fight over the last remaining resource in northern California logging country. "Our position has not been to side with one or the other, but to reveal the kind of complex human web that underlies that. Fear." Though there is dramatic value in the conflict that sets up sides, the artist's real focus is the humanity of the situation. Schirle's description reveals the artist's curiosity and relentless spirit of inquiry.

The Dell'Arte artists use the phrase Theater of Place to articulate their artistic connection with their own geopolitical community. Their notion of "theater created by, for and about the area in which you live" applies aptly to several of the ensembles in this study. However, as provocative and valuable as this concept may be for some, it is incomplete or inaccurate for others.

For Rosalba Rolon, artistic director of Teatro Pregones, the art of her ensemble is the continuous exploration of a popular and accessible aesthetic, the development of style that comes out of a long-term artistic investigation of the culture and life realities of their Puerto Rican and Latino audiences and the creation of "innovative and challenging theater rooted in Puerto Rican traditions and popular artistic expressions." Given the unfixed geography of Latinos in the United States, some experts use the term "translocal" to describe the community that Rolon understands as theirs. According to site visitor Arnaldo López, "Latino communities ... are never altogether of one place. The ties that bind will draw them in many different directions, pull them towards more than one home." It is particularly revealing that López observes, "Making community will often entail travel." That is true for Pregones' audiences, who travel long distances to see performances at the theater in the South Bronx and it is true of the company itself which tours widely in the Northeast and around the country, always seeking to ["make community" with Puerto Ricans and Latinos wherever they may be living.]

Likewise, for the members of WagonBurner Theater Troop, their theater is a momentary event that draws together a community of people who are displaced. WagonBurner ensemble members themselves live in different states and only come together to make their work. [They are bound by their histories, their traditions and their desire to make work but not by their places of dwelling.] The event of their theater becomes a place itself, a place where community can be made. Similarly, when Pregones member Jorge Merced describes his ensemble as providing a "space for [audiences] to pursue their own questioning," he inadvertently flips Dell'Arte's Theater of Place around to the place of theater and expands the idea into a space that is both physical and metaphysical.

This notion of the interconnection of imaginings between the play and the audience in the place/space of performance is a common thread amongst all these ensembles. For all, the event of performance is a moment of community that is both known and new. An important finding of this project, reflected in several of the ensembles, is that [community may exist in tradition and spirit, but it is made and remade, a constructed result of the artistic process.] In this sense, "community" is that coherence, that belonging, that specific social and aesthetic reality which is produced intentionally by the people coming together in acts of imagination.

The art of these ensembles is to create images from the audience's own experiences, histories and traditions that provide the possibility of such moments.

Community is not necessarily a given but it may be made through acknowledging and/or celebrating a sense of common heritage or place that emerges in the event of live performance. That is where the art of the making comes in. Community is a protean thing that both reflects and creates agency.

Ron Short describes Roadside Theater's ability to conjure community by allowing story to cede the singular authority of the expert individual (the playwright or author) to the power of multiple voices in the disenfranchised communities of central Appalachia:

> When you live outside of those boundaries you don't have any of that political control, that economic control, even the control of your own image. Somebody else is controlling and telling you who you are. Then the only thing that you have is your own story. That's about the only thing that you have. It comes down to how do you use that in a public way. That's essential to me. Theater is the last public forum for common people. We still can have access to it. You don't have to have the technology of television. It is a place where common people, everyday people, can get up and speak their mind and have other people listen to them. That process of dialog with the audience enters into the collective consciousness of that community and helps shape that community. As it uses the collective knowledge, it gets built together.
>
> For me, that's what grassroots theater is. It's about having a voice. A public voice. One which demonstrates not only, "This is what I think and feel," but, "I'll speak it in the public forum and then I'll wait for a response so that we can have a dialog about that." We can continue then to formulate our thoughts and change and grow as we need to in our own community.

Short's imagery of entering into the collective consciousness suggests the resonance of theater that Dell'Arte member Michael Fields describes as reflecting "back and forth." Linda Parris-Bailey, artistic director of Carpetbag Theatre Company, frequently talks about "giving back" to the community. Not only does this phrase imply the strong sense of historical obligation to home communities expressed by many educated black people, it defines the ensemble's sense of its part in an artistic and cultural exchange with its community. In hearing and retelling stories, in giving and taking through their art, Carpetbag both reflects and defines cultural identity. It is in this resonance between artist and community that the art of these ensembles thrives.

Nowhere is this resonance between the artist and the community (and the artistic organization and the community) more clear and more powerful than in the performance of "Agents and Assets" as witnessed by Los Angeles Poverty Department site visitor Ferdinand Lewis. This show was scripted directly from the transcripts of a Congressional hearing on CIA involvement in crack cocaine sales in California. It is easy to imagine with Lewis the powerful "irony of hearing the words of educated, skilled politicians spoken by actors who at some point in their lives were casualties of the Wars on Drugs." Lewis reports that "it was the act of witnessing an event so fraught with contextual weight that produced emotion" in the audience. Lewis' report suggests the issues of justice and the dynamics of power were present in the bodies and voices of the performers and accessible to the audience, not because of virtuosic impersonation of character but by the artful collision of dissonant cultures and conflicted contexts. These collisions are a known reality of the audience Lewis witnessed, consistent with the life experience, and at the same time the play unveiled truths through the otherwise entirely remote political hearings. This is exactly what Jump-Start's Steve Bailey meant by "aesthetics are politics and politics are aesthetics." Judging by Lewis' accounts of audience response and the responses of the actors themselves in their own interviews, the event of "Agents and Assets" is exactly the resonance of art that Ron Short says "enters into the collective consciousness of that community and helps shape that community."

Audiences from the communities of this study have a clear understanding of this relationship, this dynamic, that is articulate and inspiring. The people interviewed reveal a reliable expertise, founded in their own experience, that is an important voice. Confirming Dell'Arte's intimate relationship with its home, Blue Lake, California, Gene Supka, proprietor of the Logger Bar down the street from Dell'Arte's theater, recognizes that the value of their plays lies in the fact that the audience from Blue Lake knows the secrets behind the laughter. Supka's imagery reaches into the substance of the comedic form itself.

Knowledge in the audience must be tapped by the comedic artist for laughter to go beyond the consequence of mere stage antics. The reciprocity of knowledge, what is publicly realized as shared but secret experience, resonating between the artist and the audience releases the theatrical event from the physical to the metaphysical and gives the art its value. Gene Supka lays this down with profound simplicity. It is a key concept in a critical dialog about all of these theaters, regardless of form and in the development of community art theory.

Specific Practices

How these concepts and approaches are practiced and what the practice actually creates depends on the artists, the communities and the projects they select to do. These eight ensembles demonstrate a range of practices that seems infinitely variable. Certainly they work with styles ranging from the ancient traditions of storytelling and physical comedy to theatrical realism, satire and parody, vaudeville and popular entertainment traditions, theatrical adaptations of other literary forms, new adaptations of classical drama and contemporary expressions of performance art. Some of these ensembles are committed to the development of a singular style, as in Roadside's lifelong investigation of storytelling. Other ensembles, however, are openly interested in the development of a diverse range of theatrical styles and forms. Jump-Start is committed to the freedom of each of the ensemble members to design and create his/her own works, allowing style to follow needs of the project and the individuality of the makers. Jump-Start work draws on material from the gay/lesbian/bi communities, African-American communities, Chicano communities and women, yet the work comes originally from an individual whose passion reaches out in specific ways. While Jump-Start's definition of community is broad and inclusive, they work in extremely distinct communities and neighborhoods, building connections and long-term relationships. The diversity of the ensemble generates diverse work. Site visitor Keith Hennessy writes about the unique values of this approach.

Much wisdom and strength comes directly from the diversity of company members who are deeply rooted in specific communities united by ethnicity, neighborhood, sexuality, art medium, political struggle, age, gender or collective vision. As a multicommunity, polycultural resource Jump-Start is also the site and inspiration of cross-community collaborations that honor specific cultural histories while engaged in the dangerous yet fertile practicing of cultural border crossing.

Despite the vast difference, there are commonalities. Regardless of theatrical style, the story as a central structuring element is one such common practice. Likewise, the dramatic event of an individual voice speaking from a group, either as expressive of the group or in opposition to the group, is often found.

Some of these ensembles develop new work based on the creative input of an individual writer. Others work collectively with improvisational performers as the base for the creative process. Yet every group is guided by a profound respect for the time and energy it takes to make new work. They do not attempt to conform to the multiproduction "season." Rather, the creative process is understood to fit within the daily routines of life. Shows are developed over months, even years. The creative processes, though widely varying, typically include complex research and communication exchange between ensemble members and all kinds of people in the community. Cornerstone uses highly practiced processes of focus groups, advisory committees and other kinds of gathered community resources. These resources provide insight, perspective, inspiration, depth and breadth of opinion and experience. They sometimes provide material taken "as is" directly into the ensuing show. Wagon-Burner invites everyone in the yard out front to come in and join a "talking circle." "We're making a play, what do you think these characters might say or do?" Everyone talks and several people record the offerings. They talk around and through issues and ideas, they echo and reinforce each other, they use complex cultural analyses, stories and humor. The next day, everyone hears what was spoken the day before and things get reconsidered, reconceived. In addition to the "talking circle," WagonBurner methods include collective writing, editing and performing. Within the ensemble everyone has a say, under the remarkably flexible guidance of LeAnne Howe, the ensemble's organizer and principle writer/director.

Several of the ensembles use various forms of improvisation in the development process, mostly used to allow actors to work "on their feet" in rehearsal. That material is then set, more or less, for public performance. As such, this type of improvisation differs quite distinctly from the forms used for public performance by comedy groups. Alison Carey of Cornerstone, John Malpede of LAPD and several of the Dell'Arte ensemble are among those in this study who are highly skilled at using improvisation in this fashion.

John Malpede uses workshops in the community as venues for development of material. What people say and do around a particular conversation or subject matter becomes grist for performance, whether the originator is a performer in the show or a contributor to it. Malpede says, in talking about his creative processes,

> You have to be respectful of and take advantage of the resources that are there. I started [by] volunteering for activists and lawyers who were active in the community. I had to learn to be in that community, how to behave and also learn the lay of the land. I kept redefining what was most important to me. Initially it was about helping out people who are already there.
>
> You have to keep your ear to the ground and be responsive to what's there. I think a lot of decisions are practical responses to what's in front of your face, trying to find the form for what's there.

Malpede understands the time it takes to work this way. He recalls, "We'd written a grant for workshops ... and I was going to make a piece about neighborhood issues. I started doing the workshops and ... it was a year before anything came out of it."

Peter Pennekamp, a longtime fan of Dell'Arte, underscores the time it takes to make this work when he points out that, while everyone knows the truths in their plays actually come out of the community, it is not by simple coincidence that the artists express it at a time and in a way that it can be heard. Pennekamp clearly respects that these plays are the result of years and years of the artists' commitment to the town, the whole community, as well as to their craft of theater making. Over time, they have built a trust that allows people to talk with them, to share private thoughts. This accomplishment represents a set of skills equal to those required to construct a play or execute an effective comedic bit of stage business.

Another commonality, besides honoring the creative process itself, is a comprehension among those ensembles specifically devoted to working with community traditions that these traditions are theirs to reinvent, as well as to respect. Story forms the basis of Roadside's methodology and is the key to their link between art and community wellbeing. Part of Roadside's work for many years has been to undo the class and regional biases in so much mainstream culture. Roadside presented a very early and very radical challenge to longstanding concepts of poverty and class in the region. Moreover, their programs and productions countered the canned versions of Appalachian life that too often stand in as representations of the regional culture. Ron Short makes us understand that such[biases are deeply embedded in theatrical forms as well as in straightforward social behavior and institutions] Roadside has devoted much of its creative effort to exposing the depth and nature of such prejudices and to creating a public place for the beautiful, real voices of the region.

Making reference to his own experience in the Vietnam war, Roadside ensemble member Short's sense of theater as "the last public forum for common people" connects the need for story to an implicit idea of outrage and resistance. Short implies that the voices of those who do not make war but are required to fight, or of those who do not control economic policy but must bear the consequences of it, can be re-bodied or re-imaged on a stage or in a performance environment. Differentiating from what he criticizes as "popular culture" or predigested commercial televi-

35

sion and other mass-produced forms that manufacture for profit a homogenized "mythos" that keeps the real stories suppressed, Short says, "And then I think there is a whole hidden world of America that people never see. And I do believe that community theater or grassroots theater is that other voice. It's that voice that never gets a chance to speak for itself or demonstrate itself in a real way."

When Roadside ensemble member Dudley Cocke makes the following brief definition of the theater, the process that got Roadside there is visible.

> [There] are two important characteristics of our theater, accessibility and commitment to place. By commitment to place we mean commitment to the people here, the culture here, the heritage here. And that commitment leads to the responsibility to make that heritage new, to reinvent it. That's what the fun of theater is.

The Teatro Pregones ensemble is made up of Puerto Rican artists who were born, raised and trained in Puerto Rico, then moved to the U.S. mixed, in near equal measure, with Puerto Rican artists born, raised and trained in the U.S., for whom English, not Spanish, is their first language.

Pregones' work is making valued contemporary art and artists out of the cultural traditions and resources rooted in Puerto Rican life. The ensemble has developed an expertise in negotiating the problems presented when creating new work out of established plays, novels, poetry, music and the traditions that permeate the many cultures they tap.

In a particularly wry application of these approaches to creating out of traditions, WagonBurner uses the Bingo game, a common form imposed on the Native gambling traditions by the dominant culture, as the anchoring dramatic structure for their play "Indian Radio Days." The ensemble members are very aware, with a kind of W. E. B. DuBois "double consciousness," of Native American identities within the white man's world. They can perceive and make visible in their theater the "edge" where the difference of given and chosen native historical communities meets the dominant system. The most provocative and powerful theme in the interviews is this understanding and constant presence of humor, laughter and critique in the collaboratively created performance work. They collect gags and antics that reveal and mock. They provide a writing/telling that helps individuals cope with difficult situations and connect to memories and cultural histories that are sustaining. And what flashes off virtually every page of the interviews is the pleasure, the fun of the process.

One particularly challenging reality for all of these ensembles that each one has discovered is that it must struggle to find balance between speaking truth so that it can be heard and not alienating people or segments of their communities. This struggle is not unique to grassroots ensemble theater. The close relationships ensemble members actually have within their communities, though, makes the struggle immediate and present in daily life. Michael Fields at Dell'Arte suggests a particularly disarming and thoughtful perception that goes a long way toward keeping that balance. He recognizes that collective collaboration is not "normal" in our society and therefore requires that constant special care be taken to make the structure and the behavior of the collective processes as "transparent" and available to everyone as possible. At one point in the interviews, talking about bringing new people into the organization, he voices this principle of transparency.

> I think in ensemble theater, in particular, it is easy to get stuck in both individual patterns of relating to each other and holding on to history and letting that determine current practice. Both of those things are dangerous. Because [Dell'Arte] has gotten larger there has been also an influx of new people working here who naturally don't understand the history and the jargon of those who carried it around. So, we needed to make the structure more transparent, more clear to people. How things work.

Reading the interviews of their audience members it is clear that Dell'Arte has worked hard to make the organization transparent within its community. It is likewise clear that they have made their art transparent, accessible and available to their community as well. This notion of transparency is consistent with the reality at Pregones where the methods of acculturation used to integrate new actors into the ensemble are the same as those the company uses to create new work. It also is consistent with the requirements of integrating the theater into the community. Ensemble member José Joaquín García, recounts a brief but telling moment he remembers, working with associate director Alvan Colon Lespier.

> ...Alvan was putting up a flyer outside the church about the show and somebody came up and said, "Que es eso? What's that?" Alvan said, "Estamos haciendo teatro. We're doing theater." And the guy said, "Que es eso? What's that?" And Alvan made these gestures, "That's when you're on stage and you go like this," he takes a bow. And when he did that I was like, "Wow, we're not talking about creating an audience, we're talking about developing, we're talking about starting a theater."

Another strategy for many of these ensembles is to work overtly on the premise that community service need not be limited to making theater or doing anything artistic. Community service can mean doing what the community needs doing – waiting on tables at the weekly Grange breakfast or partnering with the SRO movement to remake buildings into suitable housing for the homeless or joining the PTA. These artists understand that they are citizens in the community. As they integrate this practice into their lives, the community recognizes them as citizens with commonly shared concerns and experiences. The process of a theater becoming a part of a community happens on many levels and through many relationships.

While each of these ensembles has become expert with a certain set of skills and practices required by its form of collaborative and collective creativity, taken as a whole these ensembles dash the conventional wisdom that the craft of theater requires singular authorship and stage direction. Taken individually, they represent a valuable spread of approaches. The interviews and commentaries of this study hold the details of this spread but certain practices call for mention in this essay.

In this regard, one simple and perhaps obvious reality of ensemble theater is that the artistic group remains the same people for long periods of time, often years. Hence, for the theater to get better, to grow and flourish, the members of the ensemble have to grow and flourish. This requires certain practices that may be more uniquely practiced in ensembles than in other theater organizations. Many of these ensembles have worked out ways for artists to talk critically about their own work, each other's work and the work of the company. Jump-Start as a whole has a contemporary theoretical inclination, formed by cultural politics, feminism and queer studies. In the interviews, there are lengthy passages that might be extracted as theoretical texts in and of themselves. Obversely, Jump-Start artists have learned not to assume that their status as artists specifically equips them for the work of community exchange. Rather, they seek training and they work with partner artists and educators to sustain community work. This idea of ensemble-member training as a part of the regular scheduled work day is common in these companies. This might appear on first glance to reflect a kind of generosity of spirit, but it is far more practical than that. Cornerstone's Alison Carey is particularly clear about this when she says, "As a writer I am a funnel, a facilitator of the process. When we start a workshop process I start by saying, 'I know nothing. We need you in this process.'" This sense of need for others with whom to make, from whom to learn, for partners, teachers, others who share in the work is expressed universally in these interviews. Some ensembles bring in outside guests with the specific agenda of learning from them. Some create collaborations with other ensembles for the same purpose.

Several of the ensembles seem to thrive artistically on mixing forms – theater and music, theater and poetry. Pregones artists talk extensively about their appreciation for these mixtures. Rosalba Rolon and Alvan Colon Lespier are especially articulate about this, referencing a multitude of Latino artists who are their guides and sometimes partners in this quest.

Linda Parris-Bailey, artistic director of Carpetbag, is likewise fascinated with the mixture of dramatic realism and communal singing. She places great emphasis on the written word and their plays have a literary quality that is often framed out in classical realism. Yet, her written words are fully woven with the parallel text of choral spectacle and dance. Carpetbag's stories are often the journey of a young person learning her/his place in the community. It is a kind of intervention, offering an imaginative place for encountering obstacles and temptations, witnessing and analyzing them, even changing through them. Yet, the dramatic progression is often accomplished through the emergence of a song sung by one or even all the cast, sometimes within the framework of the narrative and sometimes in an entirely presentational intervention. There is room, then, for lyrical departures from the dramatic action that intensify the theatrical event. This kind of formal eclecticism is also favored by WagonBurner, Cornerstone and LAPD.

Results of the Work of these Ensembles

A profound consequence of these approaches and practices is that these ensembles are deeply and essentially affected, even shaped by their communities. Some have brought theater forms to the community and allowed those forms to be reinvented, reconceived, transformed by the artists' interaction with the community. Others have chosen their form directly out of the traditions of the community itself. This formal cooperation between artist and community is far more fundamental a relationship than what subject a particular play chooses to undertake. The form itself is a consequence of an artistic trust in the community. Then, with this trust as common ground, the artists and the community are able to open an artistic dialog about subjects that matter, that have the community's attention and interest as an active ingredient in the performance event itself. Yet none of these artists have given up their own integrity, their own vision. In fact, this relationship lies at the core of the many visions of these ensembles.

There is also no doubt that these communities are affected in a long-term fashion by the presence and the artistic expressions of these ensembles. Some recognize that the way of life in a community has been expanded, perspectives and understandings changed. Others have found their own resources to create and build anew, in response to the work of these ensembles. A dynamic present in all these ensembles is the understanding that "helping" is an artistic function that involves making one's expertise available to another without seeking control or imposition of one's own vision. Repeatedly, community partners see these ensembles as having led them to their own discoveries. Marilyn Maxwell, the director of the Mountain Laurel Cancer Research and Support Center, thinks that storytelling and theater that she and her staff have created, out of a series of workshops with Roadside, is of critical importance to the vision and dream for their center. She says,

> ... I mean, we've got our information and education component and we've gotten that funded. We've got a cancer help system. We've got the University of Virginia's College at Wise that got a grant funded with some staff there. ... But what we think is the soul of the whole thing and if we've lost it we have lost our soul, is the theater and storytelling component. We think that is what grounds us in the community. That is what makes us human. That is what makes us reach out and try and be inclusive. It is that tool of the theater.

A year after WagonBurner's LeAnne Howe led a month-long playwriting workshop at Sinte Gleska University in the Rosebud Reservation, Liz Hopkins and Nancy Whitehorse were rewriting and restaging their own plays for a tour to other Native American communities in a multistate region. Similarly, from the evidence of this study, it can perhaps be said that Carpetbag's greatest success in its 31 years, greater even than its many productions, is the rolling wave of creativity its performances and workshops have set in motion. Like WagonBurner and Howe, Parris-Bailey and Carpetbag have had the wisdom and the aesthetic to move the collective energy of the community to the center of their work.

Yet, in the face of the acts of imagination accomplished by these ensembles, for which we may cheer as small revolutions, Steve Bailey at Jump-Start speaks with experienced wisdom. When Hennessy asks Bailey to talk about how Jump-Start tries to affect the community, the answer is typically complex: "...I don't even like that terminology. There is a way to make an exchange with the community. And for me that is what it is about, because we are learning as much as we are teaching."

Bailey analyzes the liberal notion that artists and educators are supposed to bring the uneducated nonartists to the table or to the theater so that they can be the objects of the production:

> Arts education people are always saying, "Get those children into your space, they are the future audience." And I say no. We are doing this work with them. ...
>
> I don't care that these kids don't come to see our work at Jump-Start. I don't care that they don't come and see the black work, the gay work, whatever – because that is not for them.

Bailey's remarks come from his own painful learning about racial and ethnic dynamics. His "not caring" is about refusing to perform a racial transaction that validates him as an artist while appearing to help a community with less privilege than his own. He is impatient with unchallenged ideas of how borders are crossed and the too frequent assumption that if people come to see a show about a particular community that they will necessarily be changed by it. He understands that change is long-term and slow and involves going to the community more than bringing audiences in. This way the attendance at a given event becomes a sign and result of conditions already present in the community.

What is going on here, in the careers of these remarkable ensembles, then, is more than their accomplishments, more than the formal maturity of their plays or the individual moments of epiphany and communal self-expression. These ensembles are setting standards of excellence that stretch beyond our conventional assumptions of theater and its function. They are practicing the skills necessary to allow a play to resonate with its community. They are documenting the ability of theater to be an active citizen, to exchange and learn with its community even as it unveils secrets. They are responding to the challenge presented to the American theater since the early 1970s that the simple presentation of a season of plays authored by nationally recognized playwrights must be overstepped so that each theater can become an actual expression of its own community. They are proving that the national theater of as richly varied a nation as we are can only be conceived and understood in multiplicity. Each community and its theater can be asked – expected – to contribute its own values and its own images. They can be held to a specific standard of excellence that these values and images are faithful to the dignity, fairness and honesty of the community from which they emerge, that they excite the community in ways that are satisfying to all partners in the exchange.

It's no big thing, really, in the large scheme of things. It's just what happens when good art resonates with the community of its source. It is something we as a nation are only just now beginning to experience: our own theaters as integral parts of our lives.

CARPETBAG THEATER COMPANY:
Cheerleader for the Revolution
By Ann Kilkelly

LINDA PARRIS-BAILEY, artistic director of Carpetbag Theater, jokes that the company calls her "the cheerleader for the revolution," and says, "We have been accused of being celebratory." Parris-Bailey leads Carpetbag with humor and political commitment in developing original works within and for their communities, self-defined as largely African-American and working-class. If cheer-leading is orchestrated, supportive performances for the home team from the vantage point of the margins, then, Parris-Bailey is, indeed, a cheerleader. Carpetbag's work also involves the analysis, critique and creation of theater that centrally concerns intractable social problems experienced in marginalized communities. From this standpoint, the art itself images the possibility of "revolution" or a "turning around" in characters' and actors' lives. Carpetbag's original plays, music and projects make complex art out of the fabric of lives in their own communities; and these performances blend change and cheerleading, social critique and celebration, in well-developed aesthetic processes that are filled with the passion of liberatory energy. This kind of revolution in the imagination of the community is undertaken in hopes of changing the historical dynamics of racism.

Carpetbag's situation parallels the stories of other relatively "senior" arts organizations that were formed in the early '70s with a decidedly alternative social and political agenda. The core work and politics are implied in the mission, which remains:

45

> To give artistic voice to the underserved – address the issues
> and dreams of people who have historically been silenced by
> racism, classism, sexism and ageism; tell the stories of em-
> powerment; celebrate our culture; and reveal hidden stories.

In Nayo Watkins' interviews with Carpetbag's company and
community members, Linda Parris-Bailey frequently talks about
"giving back" to the community. Not only does this phrase
imply the strong sense of historical obligation to home communities expressed by many educated black people, but it also
defines the company's sense of their part of an artistic and cultural exchange with a community. The exchange implies more
than art making as service; in giving and taking stories, in sharing responsibility for educating young people, the theater group
both reflects and defines cultural identity.

Discovery of Artistic Practice

Carpetbag makes performances from individual stories, from
family experiences and from historical events in African-
American traditions. Often their process involves the research of
listening and questioning community members about their memories of particular events relevant to both historical and present
concerns. "Red Summer" was created as a response to the
Knoxville race riots of 1919, and many of those interviewed
remember it as a signal event in their own experience. "Dark
Cowgirls and Prairie Queens," Parris-Bailey's signature piece
about black women in the American west, blended historical
research with contemporary experiences. Recent works "Nothin'
Nice" and "Swopera" focus on social and economic pressures
experienced by African-American youth. Many of those interviewed note that Carpetbag addresses the profound absence of
plays about or by black people, women, poor people, and kids.
And while the plays do treat historical and signal events around
race, gender and class, the register of the events is in the individual experience framed in an understanding of systemic issues.
Parris-Bailey is clearly a director/playwright in a somewhat tradi-

Linda Parris-Bailey, Stephen Lynn, Carlton "Starr" Releford Zakiyyah Modeste, Joseph Woods, Whitney Blue, Ajeet Daur Khalsa, Omar Abdel-alem, Jeffrey L. Cody, Nancy Prebilich and Sylvia Ruppert in "Nothin' Nice"

tional sense, in that she places great emphasis on the written word, and the plays, especially the early ones, have a literary quality that is often framed out in classical realism. Yet her written words incorporate and evolve from collaborative processes and they are fully woven with the parallel text of choral spectacle and dance. There is multiple authorship and strong leadership; they make side-by-side aesthetic spaces for historical representation and critical commentary.

Raging Fireball

Carpetbag Theatre is artist-centered, and company members describe experiencing an awakening to vocation in their first experiences with the company. When Watkins asks him for a favorite story, company member and technical director Jeff Cody

47

tells a story about former company member and founder of Café Noir, Margo Miller:

> She [Margo Miller] got into Carpetbag and she embraced the mission statement, and she was working part-time in the pharmacy department at K-mart. She got so into the mission statement that, on top of the other experience that she had, she got into working for diversity and empowerment. She just became a raging fireball. She has picked up so many tools and so many new things and has evolved them into her own. She has surpassed everything so that her association with Carpetbag has really motivated her to be somebody who we are going to go in the future, "Oh! Margaret Miller –" in the history books. It's the whole thing with her being into computers and stuff, too. She's going global.

I think that, for many artists, the discovery that political and social commitments can be addressed in art making is a signal moment, one that connects individual identity to a particular community and confers legitimation on the passion for art making. This passion for the art itself is a strong characteristic of Carpetbag's work; the joy in the making, in the individual's discovery that her/his own material has an interest for others.

Cody's story also reveals his own deep commitment to the mission. Cody has been with the organization since 1976, and has worn what he calls two hats, those of technical director and financial manager, although he has often performed and has been a researcher and collaborator throughout his association with Carpetbag since 1976. Like Miller, Cody learned many practical skills in the necessity of keeping Carpetbag together. This flexibility, or demand for multiple skills, Cody sees as part of Carpetbag's ability to survive for more than 30 years. Carpetbag's model allows for, even requires, hands-on, experience-based learning that occurs as the situation requires it. As in many small arts ensembles, the practical necessity of doing anything that needs to be done turns out to be a catalyst for the development of human resources. The relative lack of capital may produce an abundance of human capital in the short term.

Most of the Carpetbag company can perform multiple jobs and often do take multiple roles, on and off stage. Yet necessity is not the only mother of invention, as artists here and in other "Performing Community" studies also relish the opportunity to try their hand at design or acting. The absence of restriction to a single role, read only as required by lack of resources, may be a serious misunderstanding of a desire for multiple roles or developmental change within an organization.

Longtime company member Linda Hill also describes her discovery of a vocation in theater during her first show with Carpetbag:

> I was a music major, and my early training is in classical bass. Linda recruited me to do some incidental music for a play called "Celebration." I did a little bass work, a little guitar work for some of the characters' movement music. And I didn't go to sleep. I had just gotten a job. I had decided that I needed to take a break from school because I was going to do damage to my transcript if I didn't get focused. I had gotten a job at Krispy Kreme Donut Company on the night shift, so that the first night of performance I had to go straight to work, work through the day. I never went to sleep. I had a milkshake for my meal – that was the only sustenance that I had until the next show. ... When we finished the last performance, I stepped off stage and I was like, "We did it! And this is it; this is what I can do. This is what I can do right on the planet."

What I really love about these stories is the palpable pleasure in the retelling of the germinal moment, a pleasure connected to possibility, freedom and self – knowledge against the backdrop of K-Mart and Krispy Kreme Doughnuts. It is hard to commit to work that earns so few "real-life" economic rewards, and harder still to believe in that work over years of struggling to find support. Carpetbag members' strong sense of the usefulness of the art in shaping identity appears to be a crucial element in company longevity. Cody often comes back to this point and to the ongoing relevance of the mission statement.

Parris-Bailey clearly sees and encourages the creative process as activist practice of life and vocational skills. In her recent "Nothin' Nice," guest directed by Bob Leonard, Parris-Bailey used the theatrical situation to stage recurring and intractable situations and potential for change in the lives of a black family.

Starr Releford, who plays the young protagonist in this piece, describes the story:

> This one is about a guy named Lone Wolf. He's 21 years old. He's an AmeriCorps worker. He has a three- or a four-year-old daughter and basically the story revolves around him, and of course his family, but mainly him. He's struggling cause he's trying to kinda be on his own, yet he is still under his mother's wing. You know how it is when the mother does want her son to go out there and be on his own – but it's kinda hard for her to let him go cause that's her son. And so it's just about life. About him adapting to his environment. Adapting to how things are going on around him, but yet there's always a conflict. He has a daughter that's growing up. He's still dealing with the baby's mother, they're not together but they communicate because of the child. And later on, he finds out his mother has cancer. All kinds of things coming from all directions basically hitting him at one time. Forcing him to deal with it, forcing him to grow up.

Clearly, Releford understands and articulates the dilemma faced by many young black men. Yawah Awala, a parent and volunteer for the company, makes a moving remark about the urgency of the connection between young actors and young characters:

> Look at this. Take a look at it and see that you do have a choice. Let's act about it, let's dance about it, but let's not actually participate in it. We can pretend like we are doing drugs, we can pretend like we are drinking, but don't actually do it because there is a downside to that.

The theater experience Awala believes to be kind of intervention. An intractable situation can be the site of "pretending" or imaginative work that is witnessed and analyzed, even changed

Carpetbag Theater Company

Location: Knoxville, Tennessee (pop. 174,000)

Ensemble members: 7

Founded: 1969

Major activities: Creation of new work; workshops; Café Noir at Knoxville College; Theatre Renaissance for Youth

Facility: In residence at Knoxville College.

Annual budget: $200,000

Community Partnerships: The Sexual Assault Crisis Center, African American Appalachian Arts Inc., East Tennessee Coalition Against State Killing, Knoxville College, Project Change, Jubilee Community Arts and The Laurel Theatre, Circle Modern Dance, Moses Teen Center, Center for Literacy Studies at the University of Tennessee, UT theaters, Friends of Literacy, Pellissippi State Technical Community College, Beck Cultural Center, Sincere Seven, Phyllis Wheatly YWCA, The Play Group, Mediation Center, UT Law School, Highlander Center, American Festival Project

Website: www.korrnet.org/carpetbg

Company Statement

To give artistic voice to the underserved — address the issues and dreams of people who have historically been silenced by racism, classism, sexism and ageism; tell the stories of empowerment; celebrate our culture; and reveal hidden stories.

with the collaboration of the players. Although the finished piece doesn't involve the audience in a literal manner, the performance encourages the imagining of other models, as the situation is left unresolved. Indeed, as Augusto Boal says, the theater is a "practice of (not for) the revolution." The environment of rehearsal and performance, unlike almost any real life environment, is physically safe and set in a representation of community and tradition. In "Nothin' Nice," Lone Wolf's story is woven with original music and dance, drawing from vernacular traditions of gospel, blues, funk and other African-American forms. Importantly, the community of the stage character and the stage family are on stage as well. Older Carpetbag members, including Linda Parris-Bailey and Burt Tanner, play out the politics of previous generations, especially the more revolutionary politics of the '70s. The onstage chorus visually links generations of African-American experiences with the present crisis of the protagonist, imaging the powerful but usually unseen social and political forces at work.

As noted by a number of community supporters, the performance of community stories validates multiple voices and perspectives, which Awala implies is a key element in self-esteem for youth and the re-articulation of community in the present. She says: "It gives children with nappy hair a sense of belonging. It gives children that want to wear their hair natural or any other kind of way ... a sense of belonging. "

Ways of Giving Back

In all its work, Carpetbag has developed an enormous and varied range of partnerships and activities and a widespread involvement with educational programs and institutions. Carpetbag has many projects and many partnerships with public schools and community organizations that serve younger children and teens. Theater Renaissance for Youth (TRY), for example, is directed by Zakiyyah Modeste. There are programs with the Zoo, the Sexual Assault Crisis Center, AIDS Response Knoxville, The Black Cultural Programming Committee, Detoxification Rehabilitation Initiative, the Coalition Against State Killing, Project Change and many others.

They have a long-term association with Knoxville College, where the group was actually founded. In a move that has already proven explosively popular, Margo Miller organized Café Noir at the college, a club for monthly poetry slams. Carpetbag also has many projects and many partnerships with public schools and community organizations that serve younger children and teens.

Although connection with schools is not explicit in the mission, it is clearly an essential form of action. "Giving back" through education ranges from programming and direct involvement with schools at all levels, to the aesthetics deeply embedded in African-American traditions and 20th-century history. There is a conscious desire for impact on the community and a corresponding development in company members. Community members interviewed assign great value to the exposure of youth to creative avenues, show enthusiasm about the presence of theater from the African-American community, and repeatedly cite the potential of performance to motivate students to go to school.

Modeste, for example, provides her definition of success:

> If they progress personally from it, … if they just learn, if they acquire a sense that they are further along with this, or they achieve projection, or they've gotten stage presence… I think that is why I am still with Carpetbag. That's why I am still guiding us in that direction, I think, because it is very deeply rooted.

The ability to affect youth in a positive way, however minimal, keeps her with the company because the work is "very deeply rooted." It is interesting that she assesses specific skill acquisition on almost any level as important because it is attached to something else that gives it importance – perhaps its context in African-American community, or in the telling of stories by others, or in the values attached to community.

Youth in the company are encouraged toward personal expression, visibility and employment, an inestimable benefit in Carpetbag's core communities, which they identify as 60 percent African-American and working-class. Many interviewed comment on the job opportunities for youth – that they can learn to create collectively, and they can use their own experiences and stories in a collaborative process that generates some kind of work experience. This is a way of "giving back" to the performers an opportunity to have their voices heard, and it "gives back" an enormous hunk of history that honors the communities it came from.

Who Is Paying

Linda Parris-Bailey frequently remarks that they always "pay something" to those who work in productions. The "Performing Communities" survey indicates that they pay all of their employees, and a number of company members, parents and supporters cite this as among the most important practices. In addition to offering young people a presence on the stage and an opportunity to generate their own work from the stories of their own lives, Carpetbag offers contracted labor – a real job with monetary value.

Yet this "paying something," as board member Dorothy Bennett considers, is not salary money, it is wage money and at a very low level of funding. Bennett says that she and Parris-Bailey have "agreed to disagree" about money, and her comment sheds light on one of the most key economic challenges:

> Linda has done this as a labor of love. A true labor of love. Making nothing. When she talks to me about money I just look at her and laugh. It isn't even of this world, when you are talking about $6 an hour. You can't even talk to work-study students about $6 an hour. Just not. If the money does not change we won't make it. We will not make it.

The chill in Bennett's comment rises from an omnipresent concern about survival. The worry and barely suppressed anger reverberates throughout the companies in the "Performing Communities" project. Carpetbag's Jeff Cody and Roadside's Ron Short make extensive comments about the inglorious history of National Endowment of the Arts funding and conservative politics. Steve Bailey writes eloquently about Jump-Start's fight against conservative forces that threatened and in part succeeded in defunding projects and organizations in San Antonio.

Bennett further worries about the absence of sufficient "giving back" from the community to Carpetbag:

> But being on the fringes, the city doesn't see Carpetbag as a value or a threat. And they have to be one. They have to have enough voting constituency that says, "We want Carpetbag." Carpetbag doesn't go out there and put out petitions to say we need 500 names to take to City Council to convince them that we should be part of the budget for recreation. To pres-

ent them in a way that is less threatening to the city fathers and to the director of the recreation program.

Most telling is Bennett's response to Watkins' question about what the community gives back:

> Bennett: Then in a different way, it impacts Carpetbag by its limited presence, by its cautiousness of a sort. The community is not an aggressive community – or an assertive community would be a more diplomatic word. The community whispers things. ...The community does not shout out words like racism, classism, homophobia. Those things are not shouted. They don't shout things like exploitation of workers. They don't shout things like de facto segregation. They don't shout things like schools filled with racism who throw children out rather than embracing children. They don't shout things like condemned, dilapidated housing. They don't shout things like overtaxation of the poor. None of those things are shouted. If the community was more pro-active, then Carpetbag could be more pro-active. But Carpetbag, to me, is limited like any other institution is limited by virtue of where they are and where the people are. And if Carpetbag were more assertive in its art presentations to the community and the kinds of programs they did with the community, I dare say, it couldn't be on this college campus.

> Watkins: Do you think that in what it does it pushes the button a little bit?

> Bennett: Sure, sure. Carpetbag is on the edge of what this community permits. Very much on the edge. And for many people it's too far out anyway. That's part of the problem. And, you know, it is not perceived by the powers and the system as – it's not the same as Clarence Brown Theatre at the university. So the university can draw 500 people to a play that talks about something that probably won't change one life in a disadvantaged community,

Bennett's comments make me wonder to what extent a company has to be responsible for organizing political action and advocating for visibility and funding at the same time. The political question engaged in is a really tough one – having defined oneself as serving the underserved, from a standpoint that understands marginality as a political phenomenon, having developed critiques of systemic politics, how does a company "present them (itself) in a way that is less threatening to the city fathers and to the director of the recreation program?"

Clearly Carpetbag has managed the nearly miraculous in this respect – they have kept their focus on direct impact and the empowerment of artists. In reading Nayo Watkins' interviews and thinking through the Carpetbag productions I have seen and read, I am aware that their successes in being about and for the communities they serve are exactly their greatest challenges. They struggle with visibility, despite their longevity and their remarkable touring profile; they and others who work with them question their ability to survive and be economically viable (that is, to pay members salaries and have sufficient resources for ongoing productions). They have very strong artistic visionary leadership in Parris-Bailey, but this in itself presents challenges for her, as she and other members must also spend increasing amounts of time developing partnerships, training and looking for constantly diminishing funding sources.

Carpetbag negotiates this systemic morass very well, yet the focus of the company has traded touring for more time at home. Jeff Cody worries about the decreased quantity of productions. And the work at home is increasingly administrative:

> All of the little stress builders. And still being able to do the project. It was much simpler when you had earned income and a grant. ...Carpetbag was headed to a certain space, to actually fulfilling the mission. It used to be you could get the empowerment rush through the organization, but still you could stop and get an individual grant to work on an individual project, and that would feed the other part of yourself. So now, that other part, the individual part, is sort of crippled in art so that you can fulfill the social part of your mission.

The Artist as Vehicle

Many of the above challenges relate to the desire to help young people create original work. There is in that an assumption that these voices, these young people have value in a broader environment that constantly devalues them. Furthermore, Parris-Bailey demands that the work be challenging and honest, requiring investment from the audience as well as the players. She describes the difficulty of simultaneously going "out" into communities and in going "in" to company and the development of individuals and the ensemble. She says, "and it really ultimately is going to take the two focuses operating simultaneously to do the level of work we are going to do." Parris-Bailey also characteristically provides the link between the use of aesthetic materials and the community good:

> Unlike any other medium in terms of the written word, theater is designed to be performed. So, in order to return to your audience, your community, whatever – in order to return the information, what you are looking for is a reality of the experiences. ... It's the word. It's the stories. It's the dialogue. ...
>
> We are very deliberate in our work, and the people that choose that connection ... want to be connected with community. They understand that it's a part of our mission that those stories are returned, returned in ways that are as honest as we can get them and also challenge us. Because some of the things that you hear in the stories are things that people have to challenge. And where do they find the will and the means to challenge?
>
> We are the vehicles through which those stories come back. What we try to do is to seek out the lessons in the story for ourselves and for the community, too.

There is a confrontational quality, Parris-Bailey implies, in the stories that come back via the artist. Like so many of the grass-roots theaters in this study, this openly change-oriented or radical intention is regarded as inextricably linked to the material itself. In crafting performance work, Parris-Bailey implies, the art is in helping the story get through, to become visible. In a sense the living, moving bodies of the actors contain untold history written into gestures and voices. The confrontation may be very different for audiences of different races, but this difference can be accommodated if the story is told with clarity and honesty.

While focused clearly on this mission of empowerment to specific groups, such work also provides the broadest audiences a broader and more complex understanding of racial, gender and class dynamics by providing complex and well-crafted stories that move and sing. The representation of even the hardest stories on stage, framed by music and community, provides an aesthetic shape and a distancing that moves the story to another place in the imagination. The distancing may be not the "objective" stance often thought of as requisite for art, but the clearing of space for reflection and reshaping experience imaginatively.

Every show I have seen by Carpetbag depicts characters in real-life dilemmas. In Parris-Bailey's "Nothin' Nice," for example, the central character faces the issues of fatherhood and his own ability to take responsibility for his actions. The young women of the play, though not the focus here, show similar conflicts. Carpetbag's treatment is unsparing about both the social and economic pressures brought to bear on these young people and about their individual responsibility to shape their own lives.

This theater work creates forms that speak about and to particular communities, patently not abstract or universal, but particular and accessible.

Systemic challenges also frame the personal challenges. Carpetbag is one of very few community-based ensembles directed by a woman of color. The double and triple stresses and challenges faced by a woman of color in the theater dealing with issues in and about the African-American community can not be over-exaggerated. English and Women's Studies professor Donna Shores realizes this as she remarks:

And part of what it says is that she has been able to negotiate a marriage, a family and a career all this time and keep their support. ... And yes, I think she says things to women, the community of women in general, if they all get to hear. I'm beginning to feel more intensely how slow we've been to pick up on all that we can do with Carpetbag. I feel sure that we could make some more women aware of her presence.

Moving Collective Energy to the Center

At Alternate ROOTS' "Focus on Community Arts South" meeting in Lexington, Kentucky, 2002, I saw a showing of Carpetbag's piece, "Swopera." With company collaboration, Parris-Bailey developed dramatic and musical material that deals with family history, homecoming and empowerment. It is the story of a family that reestablishes its roots by building a poetry café where its soul-food restaurant once was. Again evident are the multigenerational aesthetic, funk and jazz music and choreography, slam poetry and a roster of young performers. The show was clearly new, wildly energetic, tough and difficult to stage in the less-than-perfect space. It prominently included a long section of poetry by the young cast members, neatly woven into the soul-food metaphor. The writing blended Parris-Bailey's characteristic wit with much less crafted or sophisticated work. On reflection, I found this evidence of an aesthetic that values a mixture of virtuosity and generosity. Not a playwrighting technique honored in written texts, but an important embodiment of how this art form remains porous to and in community.

The night after the close of a late-night cabaret that followed the performance, younger Carpetbag members did a series of impromptu solo performances, one after another. In the slam-poetry mode, piece after piece delivered an unimpeded chunk of each one's experience, performed with exuberance and practiced skill. The others sat in a semi-circle close to the performer, leaning forward, absorbed, many of them mouthing the words to all the pieces. Many ROOTS elders sat in the circle, cheering this evidence of a new generation with empowered phenomenal voices.

In the performance and the talkback, Parris-Bailey and several of the younger company members talked about the show. They were still fresh, very excited and very engaged with the artistic structures of the work.

Parris-Bailey and Carpetbag have had the wisdom and the aesthetic insight to move the collective energy to the center of its work. Pleasure and empowerment come from the staging of community stories, from music with deep roots in community traditions, and each story potentially generates more stories and more pleasure, perhaps Carpetbag's greatest success in its 31 years is this rolling wave of creativity its workshops and performances set in motion. We should all cheer these acts of the imagination as small revolutions.

It seems appropriate here to give Linda Parris-Bailey the last word, in which she addresses the critique of CBT as being too much in the positive:

> If you don't show people the way to the victory then what are you doing retelling the story? Its like John (O'Neal) said about telling the story to make oneself better, or telling the story to make the community better. There is a difference between a storyteller and a liar. So, we're trying to be storytellers, not liars. The importance of that relationship is key. It reshapes the story. If we are not getting to the truth, ... there is feedback from the community. Now, the community sometimes is challenged and needs to be challenged, and sometimes they don't like that. But that's all a part of how we all grow. So, it's not that we have to constantly please, what we constantly are working for is to strike the familiar in terms of what the community has told us and return it to the community.

An Excerpt from "Nothin' Nice"

By Linda Parris-Bailey

CAST:

LONEWOLF: An Americorps worker. Twenty-one years of age. He has one daughter, Kesha who lives with her mother.

VICTOR: Lonewolf's uncle. He is a Vietnam Vet, community organizer and wise man. He is in his mid-'50s.

LIL: Wolfee's mother. She is in her mid to late forties, hard working and honest about her feelings. She and Wolfee are very close.

NICOLE: Kesha's mother. Nineteen years of age. A beginning poet. Nicole works and goes to school.

KESHA: Daughter of Wolfee and Nicole, a toddler.

TYRA: Nicole's best friend.

MAYLENE: A musician (bass) Retired army nurse. Maylene served in Vietnam, came back a healer.

ACT I, SCENE 1

LIL:

I wasn't born here. I was born in Alcoa. Most people who know the name Alcoa don't even know its in Tennessee, but that's were I grew up. My father's people came from Alabama back when Alcoa was recruiting in the deep south for men to do the work in the pot rooms, stoking the fires and doing whatever else they couldn't get white folks to do. My mother's people were straight out of the mountains. Been there since the days of the Underground Railroad. Her family came out of the mountains when the Tennessee Valley authority took their land to build dams. They never really were the same off the land, my mother says. They weren't forgiving people. They were some no-nonsense people who did things their way. My mother stopped talkin' to me when Jerry and I decided to get married. That hurt doesn't have anything to do with racism. If you knew how I was raised you'd think I was a lot older than I am. I lived part of my life in the country. I'm only 47, but I grew up with an outhouse and cooked on a wood stove at my grandmother's. I grew up in a place where everything that happened, happened ten years after everywhere else. Then I moved here. And everything happens with the rest of the country, but then it happens again ten years later.

(LIL'S MUSIC PLAYS AFTER HER OPENING
MONOLOGUE)

Will you miss me

Will you miss me, miss me when I'm gone

Will you miss me

Will you miss me when I'm gone

(repeat)

(Victor's music begins. It is a funky, up-tempo, sampled rhythm that leads Victor to respond with a statement about sampling.)

VICTOR:

Maylene!! Hey, Maylene!! How come you gotta share everything you do with the whole neighborhood? Ain't no use in you tryin' to play that HIP HOP shit! IT ain't part a nothin' we understand. Them kids know you too damn old to play with them!

MAYLENE:

You don't understand nothin' after 1975!! I'm samplin' fool.

VICTOR:

Why'n't you sample something that means something and stop messing up my environment. You better start samplin' some old school, Curtis Mayfield, Donny Hathaway, Sly, War. (He starts to sing.) War WHOO, what is it good for, absolutely Nothin'! You better put somethin' on these kids. Out here on the streets no job, no money, trashin' everything in sight ... Hey whyn't you sample this We bring more than a paycheck to our loved ones and families, We bring more than a paycheck to our loved ones and families (continues to sing as the bass picks up the melody and plays under his opening dialogue) When I was young back before the war started takin' things from me, back before the first freedom songs, I fished the Bayous. Walked out my back door and down the road whenever I got ready. Free, open space. Then they brought storage tanks and put them between us and the water. Then they went from house to house buying us out block by block. Finally all of our neighbors were gone and we were left there with the tanks. I couldn't even see the water. So I left. When I came home, I didn't recognize that water. Water would shimmer blue metallic like in a Dali painting. My dog drank that water one afternoon ... he died.

LONEWOLF:

First you gotta know who's environment you talkin' about. My environment is my kitchen, cause that's where I spend my time. I eat there, I listen to music and my mamma there. My baby gets fed there. Now Kesha, that's my heart right there. She's the only thing that I worry about when it comes to my environment. She's the only thing I see when I look into the future. She wasn't what I'd call the product of family planning, but she came just at the right time to get my head together. I don't know what I was doin' out there. My moms was like, "Get a job! You ain't in school and you ain't doin' nothin' 'round here!" Yeah right, Mom. Hey, I'm young, I got time. I had six months to get ready for Kesha. Her mamma was sixteen. I was only eighteen! I was thinkin' about sex, like the survey says 27 times or more a day. My mamma was shocked when she heard that. You know that men think about sex somewhere on average of about 27 times a day! Frankly I thought that was a low estimate. She said that she understood the term "dick head" after that.

LIL:

And every Dick Head should be blessed with a daughter so he can think about the "Dog in me"!

LONEWOLF:

That's a low blow, Moms.

LIL:

That's the truth, Wolfee. I swear, I don't know how ya'll get anything done at all! If it wasn't for birth control..

LONEWOLF:

Awright, Moms. Point made, point taken. There ain't nothin' toxic about my kitchen. No, only thing toxic in my kitchen is my mamma's chittlins on new years. When I walk out my door goin' to work in the morning, I see my environment. Neighbor didn't pick up his trash, wino left his calling card right under my bike tire, and I got to tread thru five inches of damn water before I can get to the curb to take the damn bus.

LIL:

I love Joycelyn Elders. I heard her the other day and she said that the biggest problem in the country today is the three "P's" Poverty, population and pollution. That's my girl! She was at this luncheon and the moderator was talkin' about how "she resigned her position." She stood up in front a all those suits and thanked the moderator for her kindness, but she said that she didn't resign her position, she was FIRED! Because she spoke her mind. Boy, read the paper sometime. Turn off the soap opera and

Ricky Lake and Jerry Springer and listen to some folks who got some sense.

LONEWOLF:

I listen to Uncle Victor. The man's read every book in the library! He knows something about everything.

LIL:

Now that is education gone to seed! The big weed spreadin' spores and makin' folks sick like rag weed!

LONEWOLF:

Why he gotta be all that?

LIL:

That man is a walkin' contradiction. Who ever heard of a hippy, Vietnam Vet, alcoholic, gardener vegetarian, who smokes, and wears leather clothes? The man spends half his life recycling his own beer cans! Yah know he's the one that talked your father into naming you Lonewolf. Everybody in the neighborhood thought it was a nickname until you went to school. Principal thought I didn't know the difference. Kept saying, "Yes, but what's his real name?

LONEWOLF:

Moms, Uncle Victor taught me to be a man.

LIL:

What kind a man, Mr. Twenty-seven times a day? What did he teach you to have on your mind? What you doin' for Kesha?

LONEWOLF:

What's her mamma doin' for her?

LIL:

Goin' to school!

LONEWOLF:

And workin' at Mick-e-dee's for minimum wage while I take care of Kesha. I'm doin' my part, Mom.

LIL:

Right up to the time you take her home to her exhausted mamma at the end of a 12-hour day!

LONEWOLF:

Why you always on her side? You women always be gangin' up on us. When we try and do good you just dog us anyway! You think takin' care of a baby by yourself all day is so easy? It ain't like I'm not workin'.

LIL:

That little piece a job at Saint Luke's ain't nothin'. What its goin' ta do for you next year? You got benefits? You got enough money to put clothes on that baby's back?

LONEWOLF:

When I leave there I'll have some carpentry skills. I can rehab a house or paint. I got more skills now than I ever had.

LIL:

But what you gonna do with those skills? Only thing a man can do with a little bit a carpentry skills is go to one a those job places where they send you out for day labor. What they call that place that opened up down the street?

LONEWOLF:

Labor World is down the street, Labor Ready is down on Biscayne.

LIL:

It's just like bein' a day worker in white folks' houses. Like your grandmother talks about when she was in Harlem. Waitin' on the corner for somebody to pick you out for a day job.

LONEWOLF:

Mom, I won't be sittin' at no Labor World lookin' for work. I know people now who will hire me after the program.

LIL:

We'll see, baby. You better check on Kesha. She probably needs another diaper change.

LONEWOLF:

I sure will be glad when she's toilet trained.

LIL:

I told ya'll she was too young for toilet training. Everybody's always in such a hurry ta get they kids grown and out the way.

LONEWOLF:

Well, I'm grown, but I ain't out your way yet!

LIL:

Brother, how I know that!

LONEWOLF:

I gotta go, Mom.

LIL:

Where you goin'?

LONEWOLF:

I got ta catch up with Victor.

LIL:

Did you forget something?

LONEWOLF:

What?

LIL:

Kesha!

LONEWOLF:

I thought you could watch her while I was gone.

LIL:

Then I guess you should'a asked me! I got a hair appointment in 15 minutes.

LONEWOLF:

Can't you take her with you?

LIL:

Wait a minute, I'm going to the hair dresser where some sister's gonna have my head under water, then a dryer, then the curling iron, and you're going to TALK to your Uncle Victor but she should go with me?

LONEWOLF:

You're her grandmother.

LIL:

And you're her father. Like LL Cool J says "all I ever wanted was a father." That man said a father, not a grandmother. That's what Kesha needs, a father. Or you think that only applies to boys? As my mamma told me "I raised mine!" I'll see yah when I get back.

LONEWOLF:

Thanks, Mom. Come on Kesha you goin' with daddy.

(Lonewolf and Kesha exit)

CORNERSTONE THEATER COMPANY:
Love and Respect at Work in the Creative Process
By Robert H. Leonard

ALISON CAREY, THE RESIDENT WRITER in the Cornerstone Theater ensemble, says she falls in love when she makes art with a community, and I take her very, very seriously. Even in these interview transcripts, I can feel her bubbling enthusiasm, her deep knowledge of what she experiences. Carey, an artist of considerable maturity, describes what it is to make art with someone. No weekend fling here, Carey is talking about the whole big deal – total immersion, no holds barred, even-steven equality, no-pretense honesty, and in for the long haul – a fully mature affair of the heart.

Okay, great, everyone can get behind falling in love, but what does that mean, in a practical sense, in terms of making the art, in terms of making those artist/community partnerships actually creative? Is it useful for me or is this just something that Alison Carey has in her soul, a connection with the goddess that the rest of us can only envy? Without getting into a Sunday sermon on love (or a psychoanalysis of the art-making processes), can we explore Carey's metaphor for its values and lessons?

In the early phases of this work, an enormous amount of energy must be spent in developing the participation of individuals from the community. Although early conversations with organizational partners – beginning as early as a year prior – will get word about the project out to individuals, this phase sometimes requires ensemble members to approach neighborhoods directly, canvassing for potential participants. Once scriptwriting is

69

underway, the same sort of street-level interaction takes place. During the script-development phase, the text is not only reviewed by community members who are in the cast and crew, but also community partners and focus groups. In some cases scripts are actually put in bars, cafes and other community meeting places, where patrons can jot notes and comments in the margins. The development strategy for a community collaboration will typically include about 20 meetings with community focus groups and community leaders. Ensemble members not only meet with community members as part of the play-development process, but throughout the production process continue to meet regularly with them.

In this brief paragraph there is a boat-load of work – intense, demanding and time consuming. The research-and-development phase for a playwright in the more conventional process (one person writing a script) can, itself, be a long and laborious task. That is to say nothing of the soul-searching work of actually writing the script, a task that has often brought the individual writer to moments of anguish and doubt. Opening these creative steps to a group process makes them significantly more complicated, at the least. Beyond mere numbers of people, Cornerstone enlists a wild mix of experience, background and skill level. People with established skills in artistic processes and little-to-no knowledge of the given community work in combination with people who have little-to-no established artistic skills but have deep knowledge of the community and all its ins and outs. While the mixture of general assets and deficits in this combination implies a kind of balance, the practice of negotiating this balance, person to person, asks for vision, patience and understanding well beyond conventional practice. Alison Carey makes a clear and important statement about this. She says, "If you do this [work] for purely selfless reasons, you're going to burn out soon." Selflessness would seem to many to be an asset, even a virtue. It is considerable experience that voices distrust of such motivations. Carey goes on,

... you can't do [a particular project] because it's morally

"For Here or to Go?" – The "Cops Chorus" made up of members of the LAPD dancing alongside community participants from the L.A. neighborhoods of Boyle Heights,
Baldwin Hills, Chinatown and Watts. Photo by Craig Schwartz Photography

appropriate. It can be true that it's morally appropriate, but
if you're in this context and you're not producing the art
that you want to produce, you're going to burn out. You've
gotta really want it for you.

At the heart of Cornerstone's process is a pragmatic conviction
that is intimately connected to Carey's imagery of falling in love.
The creative process must feed everyone, artist, community
member and audience alike. Carey makes the richness of this
principle particularly clear when she says,

> People come to this not because they have things to keep to
> themselves, but because they have things to share. As a
> writer I am a funnel, a facilitator of the process. When we
> start a workshop process I start by saying, "I know nothing,
> we need you in this process." What the hell do I know? I
> think that the community members take being needed in the
> process very seriously and they realize quickly that their role
> in the process is very valued.

Desire, need and satisfaction are three elements of love that are
essential to both the love-making and creative processes. Being

71

needed, being recognized and valued for one's intrinsic assets, this is understandably elemental for healthy relationships. What calls on us for fierce discipline is that these same elements can mask unhealthy relationships – in art making as in love partnering. When the partnership is out of balance, in terms of power or dependency or ultimate worth, then an unhealthy element creeps in. For example, one cannot love in order to change someone. The negotiation does not go that way. This distinction between differing intentions seems critically important to plumb.

Cornerstone has gained considerable insight into this matter, mostly based on the ensemble's careful understanding of the nature and intent of well-considered artistic partnerships. Bill Rauch, ensemble member and artistic director of Cornerstone, and a co-founder with Carey, speaks about the function of art with blunt clarity.

> You cannot predict what art changes. You're naïve if you think you know how you're going to change the world with the art you create. It's equally naïve and irresponsible even to acknowledge that art changes the world. ... The artist is creating an image of the world, and that shapes how people see the world.

As important as "shaping how people see the world" may be, and Rauch thinks the act of making art is quite important, Cornerstone is becoming more and more aware that the key to their work is in their art, not in the change that may follow out of their art. Carey says,

> Our primary job is to create good plays, and if we did a crappy play for a very diverse audience, we would have failed. To say you have to keep the art first would be a false dichotomy. Oxygen is first, but you can't go three days without water. Our art doesn't exist without the way our art is created and the involvement of the community, and the involvement of the community wouldn't work with bad art. We used to get questions in the beginning: "Are you art or social work?" We're not either of those things. It can look like social work on the outside, while it's actually a

way of making the kind of art that's most satisfying to us. There's no way that we would have lasted this long if that weren't the case.

Cornerstone's clarity that their success is based on making art that satisfies all partners involved in the process is one of considerable maturity. Many cultures within the U.S. openly celebrate the values of love and family as forces for cohesion and progress. Nonetheless, it is commonly understood that loving someone in order to make them different, to change them, is a recipe for disaster. The foolish youth who would cleanse the tarnished soul of another is one such story-line. Likewise, those of worldly knowledge who would lead the innocent into maturity (Henry Higgins and Eliza Doolittle) are always doomed. The concept of the quiet enabler in an addictive or abusive family is a grim reminder of how destructive these unbalanced relationships can get. Yet many of our institutional systems would like to dredge up justifications for support of the arts based on the very suspect criteria of how art might change society.

In his interview with the director of education at the Denver Center Theater Denver, Daniel Renner, as well in his own reflections, Ferdinand Lewis gives considerable thought to how pernicious this trend could become. He rightfully raises the alarm that the National Endowment for the Arts might pursue what seem to be its own intentions toward outcome assessments.

There is a trend in art-support systems to quantify the impact of art, even in the conventional forms of plays by playwrights performed by actors in playhouses. Finding out how many people come to the show, how many "new" people, etc., would seem to be a way of evaluating the health of the arts organization, at least of its function as an income-producing mechanism. It gets confusing, though, and sometimes blatantly misleading, when it comes to evaluating the art itself. In evaluating art that is directly connected with community, art that is built out of community collaborations, there is the temptation to point to the good that comes of it. People seem to want to justify the effort according to some long-term, tangible value that returns to the community for the investment that it makes in the creative process. The trend toward quantitative evaluation really gets pumped when it comes to how art may or may not affect social change. Once the claim is made, the desire to prove it seems to come right along behind.

Through all the trends and social imperatives, Cornerstone stands as a beacon of responsible creativity. Alongside the love-affair analogy, another word surfaces in the ensemble's thinking as critically important: respect. Bill Rauch uses respect as a core value for the work of the company, a guide for partnerships. In his interview, Rauch offers a couple of anecdotes about working with members of a community:

> For auditioning, for instance, we ask what are the places we must audition. We present to them how we build a project and they tell us how to best do that, most respectfully for that community. [Lewis interjects that respect seems to be integral to the Cornerstone process, not just a needlepoint motto.] For instance, when we did a collaboration with the Chinatown community here in L.A., we wanted the word "drag" in the posters for the project, but the word, it turned out, had all these different connotations in Chinatown. So this becomes a dialogue with the advisory committee.

Two major criteria held by Cornerstone as measures for success emerge out of the imagery offered in these interviews by Carey and Rauch: respectful ways and art that satisfies its many participants. It is in that context that Carey asserts that she "needs" her community partners. It is in this context that Rauch says, "The company's aesthetic is to include the community's dialogue with itself in the script, which calls for opposing voices and layers of meaning and a vital richness. Multiplicity of viewpoints: It's essential to our mission." He is careful to add, "I think a lot of people stop at the 'multiplicity of voices' thing, and interpret it as 'Can't we all get along?' – a kind of superficial multiculturalism. But including the voice of the oppressor along with the voice of the oppressed is a very strong political stance."

While a "multiplicity of voices" may offer a strong political stance within the art and in the context of the particular commu-

---

Cornerstone Theater Company

Location: Los Angeles, California (pop. 3,700,000)

Ensemble members: 18

Founded: 1986

Major activities: Creation of new work; workshops; internships, fellowships; @ Traction Performance Series; annual community arts awards; commissions; Cornerstone Institute.

Facility: Rents space in downtown Los Angeles; performs in community and public spaces all over town, LORT and other theaters nationally.

Annual budget: $1 million

Community Partnerships: (selected) Casterlar Elementary, Watts Village Theater and the Watts Towers, National Conference for Community and Justice, East L.A. Community Corporation.

Website: www.cornerstonetheater.org

Company Statement

Cornerstone Theater Company is a multiethnic, ensemble-based theater company. We commission and produce new plays, both original works and contemporary adaptations of classics, which combine the artistry of professional and community collaborators. By making theater with and for people of many ages, cultures and levels of theatrical experience, Cornerstone builds bridges between and within diverse communities in our home city of Los Angeles and nationwide.

---

nity, Rauch also is careful to make a distinction between thoughtful, respectful, powerful art and social service. He states,

> The social-service aspect is often overstressed. In fact we have deliberately stopped emphasizing that. The majority of communities that we work with are lower income and don't have access to professional theater, that's true, but the work is just as much about what we are learning as artists: It's a mutual exchange. ... Even colleagues can misunderstand, thinking that we do this just for the social service, but the fact is, we do it to create the best art that we know how to create.

With these principles of respect and mutual satisfaction held central in their work, Cornerstone has been able to reach toward an equality of partnership that is consistent and productive. It must be said unequivocally, however, this equality of partnership is elusive – as difficult to establish and maintain in the creativity of an artistic relationship as ever it may be in the amorous ones. Over the years, Cornerstone artists have learned and developed some reliable methods and approaches for keeping the balance of equality in their partnerships.

One primary element in their work is the "advisory committee," a group of community members who are brought together at the very conceptual beginning of projects and continue throughout. Bill Rauch has some very interesting things to say about the advisory committees and the processes that surround them.

> We build a community advisory committee from the community, and sometimes they're active and sometimes they aren't. They usually have various levels of input. But this committee provides guidance. ... [It] helps to translate for you, literally and metaphorically, in terms of issues and code words in the community and whether you're pushing a button without even realizing it. ... The committee is also important for the legacy of the project. What will be the ongoing impact after the project is over? The advisory committee has plenty of thoughts on that.

The implied processes of selection and inclusion are many and varied. No doubt Cornerstone has had committees that don't come together, don't bond with the project, but over the years Cornerstone has found that the vital dialogue and dynamic energy that is released through the advisory committee are essential elements in the creative process. Sometimes an advisory committee reactivates after the completion of the show itself:

> For instance, the Watts Village Theatre Company started out of the project we did in Watts, and Cornerstone's managing director is a board member of Watts Village. During the "road years," [before the company settled in Los Angeles] we would donate money [through the advisory committee] for the community to start a theater. Recently, by the way, one of them sent a $500 check to say thank you. In Los

Angeles, we measure a broader range of impact, rather than just helping to leave a theater company behind us. People call us for help with college applications, or to borrow sound equipment. Often, community members stay active with the company long after the project ends.

When asked about how a project actually starts at Cornerstone, Rauch went again right to the matter of how a project is partnered within the community.

It could start from ensemble members talking about an issue they have a hunger to work with, or someone from a community approaching us, or else we could just start with an idea and find the market for it. Usually, it's about one person in a community making the leap of faith and becoming an advocate for the project. Over the years we've had a lot of projects die because they couldn't find that advocate. That's true in every project, finding that person.

Working then from a base of connection with the community through the individual advocate and the advisory committee, Cornerstone continues the cooperative collaboration in the creative processes. These artistic techniques are only as equitable as their organizational structures. Lewis notes in his field notes that Cornerstone's attention to and competence in organizational structure is essential for the artistic processes to flourish.

Rauch and Carey both have much of value to say about Cornerstone's artistic approaches and methodologies. They offer many exercises and procedures that allow for the generation of material from the community and the playing back of that material for the community during the development process. Variations of improvisation and creative writing exercises are common to their process. Cornerstone often uses the focus group as a methodology for starting discussion or dialogue around the subject of the project. Perhaps others might use what they call story circles for similar purposes. It might be an interesting study to compare these different methodologies that mix community members with ensemble members at the developmental level – their formats and procedures, the details of their protocols. They would all presumably identify story, opinion and experience as their ultimate point of interest.

When asked about this kind of detailed exercise and script development technique, Carey responds with wonderful specificity.

> A lot of them are essentially improv stuff up on your feet, but I also focus a lot on writing and just talking. I use simple stuff like people writing down what are three smells of your community and what are three sounds of your community? As the playwright, I need to think about those things that other people take for granted; it's a way to get them to not take the community for granted. I do so many adaptations, so you're looking at the core of the play. but in the context of the community. If a moment in the play is about, say, "hiding," it's practical to find out where a person would hide specifically, but also what would make you hide. We spend time just free-writing, like giving people a starting sentence like, "I woke up this morning and I..." and then passing the papers around and everybody writes, then everybody passes their papers and then you have to respond to that story. You get these wild expressionistic stories. That just gets people talking.

This is exactly the kind of deep investigation that evens the partnership. The writer is working directly with her partners from the community in an open flow and interchange. Cornerstone, unlike some of the other companies in this project, often works with previously scripted material they adapt through their partnerships so that the material has direct and immediate presence and reference, not simply thematic relevance to the community. That is why Carey suggests that the play might be about hiding, and she is looking for how hiding in the play connects with hiding in the particular community.

When asked for other examples of how she might adapt exercises to the themes of a play Carey refers to a project called "The Good Person of New Haven." In this project Bertolt Brecht's play, "The Good Woman of Setzuan," was adapted through a Cornerstone collaboration with specific communities in New Haven, Connecticut.

In one exercise a person would write to an imaginary grand-child why they've been a good person that day, and pass that to the person on one side of them, then write down why they were a bad person that day and pass that to the person on the other side of them. Then we can talk about what it's like to have people know you as both a good person and a bad person. You sit down in a circle with a group of people and do a writing exercise and that's a spring-board, a starting point for a conversation. I always go in there with a plan of what I'm going to do and have to change it, because every group is different.

Carey explains that sometimes words from community members find their way directly into the script exactly as spoken.

It depends on if I have a lot of time with people. It's gener-ally not that, though, because there's not enough time with people to get specific, but it definitely happens when some-one does something and you say "that's perfect." But I'll tweak what someone has done. I do my best to credit peo-ple all over the place and I would write very bad plays if I didn't have all this input. In "Steelbound" [a project adapt-ing "Prometheus Bound" in the context of the end of the steel industry in Bethlehem, Pennsylvania], there were pas-sages that were word-for-word or moment-for-moment from what someone told me of his experience, and I talked with him about it and he was fine.

In this same project in Bethlehem, working in collaboration with Touchstone Theater Company, the script was distributed in bars and restaurants, so that people could "scribble things in margins" as a technique for interchange during the development phase of that script. It is such an audacious notion for a play-wright, working within her own passionate creativity, to seek this kind of open collaboration. Rauch puts the matter into a whole picture.

Here are people who are bringing themselves together in combination with professional actors, transforming them-selves into this very dynamic combination. There's some-

79

thing aesthetic about the variety of ages and body types and life experience, a diversity that is part of the fabric of the work, and that's what makes it powerful.

This is entirely consistent with their mission that states, "Cornerstone builds bridges between and within diverse communities." As Lewis observes in his field notes, Cornerstone not only builds such bridges as part of the processes to make their shows, they often become a bridge themselves, providing the structure for people to move, change and grow "between and within diverse communities."

Altogether then, from artistic techniques to organizational structures, Cornerstone Theater demonstrates a career-long commitment to equality in artistic partnerships with communities. This equality in the creative process is carried out with the use of many techniques, some highly unusual, some typically conventional, but always intended to release the "the best work possible." This equality is maintained and vitalized by a career-long commitment to the deceptively simple and deeply demanding values of love and respect. Values, processes and methodologies that the interviews of this project reveal are practical, pragmatic and accessible to those who would take on the discipline and rigor they demand.

An excerpt from "Steelbound"
By Alison Carey

PROMETHEUS:

I'm a steelworker. Steelworkers don't consult.

HERMAN:

So you'd rather just stay here? Chained like you are?

(PROMETHEUS nods.)

Not me. I think this place is kind of scary.

PROMETHEUS:

This scary is my scary. I know this fear.

HERMAN:

It's almost like you like it.

PROMETHEUS:

You wouldn't understand.

HERMAN:

Don't blame me for that.

PROMETHEUS:

Then I'll blame history. The rolling mill of history
That squeezed me down and pushed me along
At all those miles an hour and then left me to rust.

HERMAN:

But it was dangerous to work here.
You know that. The heat, the light, the fire,
The asbestos, the sulfur, the ammonia, the cyanide,
The steam, the smoke, the graphite, the falling scale,
The chromium, the molten metal, the cranes, the flying
And spinning beams, the trucks, the splinters,
The, the everything.
Don't shave, your beard protects your face!
Put on your dust shields, your gloves, your leggings,
Your wooden shoes with conveyer belt rubber soles!
Careful of the burns down the back of your throat,
The sandy, burned eyes of welding flash,
And the headaches for three days from the epoxies!
Can't keep all the bells and whistles straight?
Too bad, but everybody still loves a Tilly switch:
"The thing still runs you over, but it stops soon after."
All that and you still get complacent,
Walking around like you're in your own bedroom.
But you still could die any minute,
Crushed in the beam yard, burned doing a reline.
The list is too long.
Look at what it did to your body.
Men weren't made for what this place
Was capable of doing to them.

PROMETHEUS:

I know everything this place was capable of
But I know the men and women
What they were capable of, too.
You have a list of words there
But I lived the list.
A ladle overrun, the spill hits the water,
Steam everywhere, graphite falling,
You can't see a thing. So you don't move,
And you hear your buddies yell, "Don't move!"

And you can feel the molten metal between your legs
And you can feel the mouth of hell has opened up
To swallow you. And you don't move.
You will never know. No one will ever know
Who didn't stand there, not moving,
What it's like when the building blocks of a planet
Reach up to take you back home with them.
You will never know.
Max said it, I think it was Max,
"Steelworkers don't have blood in their veins,
They have steel." How can I go back
To just having blood in my veins?

HERMAN:

I've only ever had blood. It's done me okay.

PROMETHEUS:

That's you.

HERMAN:

I guess so.

PROMETHEUS:

I'm tired.

HERMAN:

Me, too. I know, I know.
I don't know tired until I've put in a triple shift
Down in the butcher shop.
I understand as best as I can, but I'm still tired.
You know, it's true:
There are some people who get satisfaction
From what's happened to you.
People who could never get a mortgage
Because they didn't work at the Steel.
People who never felt they had a job for life

Because they didn't work at the Steel.
People who never knew that they belonged somewhere
Because they didn't work at the Steel.
People who always worried about their kids
Because their kids wouldn't work at the Steel.
There's not many in this world who had everything
Like the people who worked at the Steel.
Most people outside never thought the world wouldn't change
Like people did who worked at the Steel.
But I'm not sorry for anything you ever had.
I'm glad you built the bridges and buildings and rockets
And so many things that make my life possible.
But I'm not sorry that I didn't get to build them.
I'm not even sorry that I'll never know what it's like
To stare down molten metal, your eyes aching,
And have the metal blink first.
Standing in the dark,
I can close my eyes,
I can hear the echoes
Of the bangs and the hisses and the yells
When I close my eyes.
I can see the shadows
Of the blues and the oranges and the glowing white.
I can smell the lingering scent of the tangy perfumes of your days.
I can taste the last acrid tendrils of smoke.
I feel the memory of the heat when I close my eyes.
When I close my eyes it warms me still.
And that's enough for me.
There's one thing I'll always be jealous of, though.
Most of the days of your lives, you knew
That the people who stood next to you
Would watch your back. You knew
The people who stood next to you
Would risk their lives to save yours.
You knew because you saw it happen every day.
Not because they had to, or because they should

But because they wanted to. Because they were proud to.
The history of this place is not just the history
Of injustice and battles,
Or accomplishment and courage,
It's the history of fellowship, of care.
And that's what you carry away from here,
Whenever you leave and wherever you go.
And it's not something I'll ever know,
Not like you do.

WOMAN WITH HOT DOGS:

There's a festival up on 4th, kids running around,
Balloons, barbecue and cold glasses of lemonade.

(The other FESTIVALGOERS enter.)

WOMEN CHORUS LEADER:

We want to be up there, and we want you to be there, too.
You need to figure out how to come with us.

PROMETHEUS:

I know where all the dead are. The famous ones
On Nisky Hill and those buried out back without a marker.
I know how they died, on the job or off,
By their own hand or their bodies failing.
I can give a tour of this plant by every place the dead
Sat or worked or ate or waited or laughed.
I miss the ones I knew and the ones I didn't.
I miss them.

HERMAN:

I bet they miss you, too,
But they never asked you to bury yourself with their bones.
Any more than you'd ask all these people give up their lives
To stay with you.

STEELWORKER CHORUS LEADER:

You say you know history.
Can't it tell us anything that'll set this man free?

YOUNG PERSON CHORUS LEADER:

He's still standing next to people
Who will risk their lives for his. We will.

(HEFFY, FESTA and UZ enter)

HEFFY (entering):

You still here?
Damn, I thought you would have had those things off
By the time we got to Nick's.

FESTA:

Think those welds are real?

UZ:

Sure, the forces of progress are pretty powerful,
But we're in the union.
We got rules against welding fellow members to things.

HEFFY:

Those two are too busy trying to ruin everyone else's life
To be back anytime soon.

FESTA:

They could come back a hundred times. It doesn't matter.
We could outsmart them a thousand.
We take care of our own.

FESTIVAL GOER 1:

He doesn't want to leave?

UZ:

Anybody tell him there's free food out there?

FESTIVAL GOER 2:

He won't leave.

FESTIVAL GOER 3, 4, 5, 6, 7 & 8 (Tugging on various adults' sleeves):

Why won't he leave?

HEFFY:

Every day I wake up and I remember
I'm not going to work where I went to work
All those years. And every day I ask myself
"Which story you going to be telling yourself today, Heff?
The one about the steel mill that accomplished things
That no one could ever have imagined possible?
Or the one about the steel mill that closed down
And ended a way of life?"
Some people are afraid
That you undercut the achievement
If you acknowledge the tragedy.
I don't think so.
I have them both with me always.
You have the right to feel whatever you need to feel
And say whatever you have to say
For as long as you want.

UZ:

If anyone says you don't,
You have them come to us.

FESTA:

But just because you have the right to be angry,
That doesn't mean you have to be angry every day.

UZ:

We don't build America anymore because we already built it.

We finished the job.
And everything we built is still out there,
Wherever you look.
And it's going to be out there a good long time
Because, after all, it's made of steel.

HEFFY:

I wish things hadn't worked out this way.
I miss the smell and the noise and the way you feel whole
When you do something as well as anyone could ever do it.
But I'll tell you a secret: sometimes, just sometimes,
I like the clean air and the quiet just fine.
Come on, brother.

(PROMETHEUS looks down at chains, then turns the chains so the welds fall off easily, but he still won't leave.)

Come on, brother.
All those years we all knew it:
The walls, the machines, this place was the body.
But we were the soul. The people. You, too. All of us.
Don't you try to tell me the soul can't go on
After the body's turned cold and lifeless.
(Looks around the empty mill.)
Don't you even think of telling me that.

THE CAST:

PROMETHEUS, PROMETHEUS,
PROMETHEUS, PROMETHEUS...

PROMETHEUS,
PROMETHEUS,
PROMETHEUS,
PROMETHEUS,

PROMETHEUS,
GOTTA COME ON OUT, NOW (2X)
PROMETHEUS,

BETTER COME ON OUT, NOW (2X)

PROMETHEUS,
CAN YOU SEE US HERE? (2X)
PROMETHEUS,
CAN YOU HEAR US STILL? (2X)
PROMETHEUS,
IT'S BETHLEHEM. (2X)
PROMETHEUS,
YOUR BETHLEHEM. (2X)
PROMETHEUS,
WE KNOW IT'S TIME.
PROMETHEUS,
YOU KNOW IT'S TIME.
PROMETHEUS,
LIFT UP YOUR HEAD.
PROMETHEUS,
REACH OUT YOUR HAND.
PROMETHEUS,
FOR BETHLEHEM. (2X)
PROMETHEUS,
YOU ARE BETHLEHEM. (2X)

PROMETHEUS,
COME OUT UNBOUND. (4X)

PROMETHEUS,
COME OUT HOPEFUL
COME OUT JOYOUS
COME OUT WISER
COME OUT FREE

PROMETHEUS,
UNBOUND
PROMETHEUS,
UNBOUND... (REPEAT INTO FRENZY)

PROMETHEUS,
PROMETHEUS

PROMETHEUS,
PROMETHEUS,
PROMETHEUS!

PROMETHEUS:

No matter how many years I worked here,
I still had to stop and watch every time the oven was tapped.
It was beautiful.
I was happy when I worked here,
And I didn't think I'd ever leave.
But here I go.

(EVERYONE looks at him expectantly. He steps away from his chains.)

So let's go.

(Blackout.)

THE END

THE DELL'ARTE COMPANY: Damn Good Theater – What It Is and How to Get It in Blue Lake, California
By Robert H. Leonard

COMMUNITY-BASED OR GRASSROOTS THEATER can be good only when it is driven by a mature theatrical philosophy. Hear "good" as: effective, compelling and appreciated. Time and again, successful theater artists within the field of grassroots theater reveal that their essential drive is to make theater. What is particularly interesting is that the reverse may also be true – artists connecting deeply with a specific community through the art form of theater may be essential to a mature theatrical philosophy. The reality of these statements could establish an undeniable and highly valuable standard of excellence for the field.

The Dell'Arte Company players put on outlandish clothes, grossly deformed noses and outrageous fat suits. They fall down a lot and tell stories about everybody in town. They make human beings out to be pretty ridiculous. They work hard to do this, practice a lot. They make it look easy.

Most people in Blue Lake, California, think Dell'Arte is crazy. A lot of Blue Lakers have come to love their clowning actors, but they still think they're crazy. After all, they started a professional theater ensemble, a permanent group of actor-artists who make their living creating and producing plays, in a redwood logging town of 1,200 on the north coast of California. Worse, when the founders of Dell'Arte moved into town in the mid-1970s, the logging industry was in a pitched battle against the national environmental movement. The logging industry provided the only jobs in Blue Lake, whether directly employing loggers

91

themselves or service and support employment of teachers, grocery clerks and barkeepers. No logging, no town. That connection was universally understood.

Right off the bat, Dell'Arte started staging jokes about the logging-environmental struggle. Here came hippies, with grants from the government, making jokes about salmon poachers and forestry agents. And they didn't get killed. And they didn't just get away with it. They became surprisingly, unexpectedly successful. Not only did they find and build an audience, they've become a pillar of the community – loved, respected and deeply appreciated. They've raised families. They've established an ensemble and an international school for physical comedy respected in all corners of the theatrical world.

Interviews with the artists in this project substantiate that their experiences – creating, researching, organizing, teaching and living in Blue Lake – are the essential foundation for a mature theatrical philosophy, which the leadership of Dell'Arte articulates as well as it practices. They center their artistic philosophy and vision on a concept they call "Theater of Place: theater created by, for and about the area in which you live." Their full statement is a vision of extraordinary standards and thoroughly practical application.

Talking about Theater of Place, Joan Schirle, co-artistic director of the ensemble, reveals just how practical this all is – how the artist makes her art.

> It is basically a mirror image of this little town that we live in. The piece we did last year included a very thinly veiled set of characters based on the Blue Lake City Council. That was made with some input from individuals, asking them to actually contribute pieces of their own dialogue, which was incorporated into the play. It was also based on what has been a dominant issue here for many years, which is the results of the use of this land over a long period of time, and what the generation now has to face, both in terms of the loss of resource and the fight over the last remaining resource... Our position has not been to side with one or the other, but to reveal the kind of complex human web that underlies that. Fear.

Dell'Arte's Mad River Festival closing ceremonies, "The Blue Lake Pageant" Photo: Sedric Nin

Schirle puts her finger right on the matter. Though the conflict sets up sides that are very real in the community and must exist clearly in the theatrical representation, the artist's real focus is the humanity of the situation. Schirle's description reveals an artist's curiosity and relentless spirit of inquiry.

In the "Korbel" series fear is at the heart of a lot of it. Fear of change. The change is inevitable. It is how a community can work together. The "Korbel" series, each year that it was done, reflected an issue that perhaps threw additional light on that. One year it brought in the idea of militias, which was a big thing in the United States that particular year. Another year brought in the idea of prejudice within the community of transgendered people, of foreign people. Then the last one we did dealt with kind of the relationship of the citizens in town to the city council. It didn't have a particular issue, it was more of an exploration of local types of people.

It is easy to imagine how the theater that Schirle describes resonates with the people of Blue Lake who are interviewed and quoted in this project. It is fascinating how the responses of the community people interconnect with the impulses and intentions of the ensemble members.

Interviews with Michael Fields, managing artistic director of the ensemble, offer insight into the practical aspects of Theater of Place. His description of a new project tells of a cross-cultural dialog that is fraught with misunderstanding. At this point in their development, Fields expresses trust in the approach and yet careful caution.

> It will be about the building of the casino here in Blue Lake. We'll follow it from ground-breaking through to operation, interviewing four or five people on video documentary over the course of the project, having Native American presentations, and then we will develop a play based on it. That is classic theater of place to me. We called it the Detalian Project. "Detalian" means the beads that were used to gamble with in the Native American tradition. The woman at the Blue Lake Rancheria, our partner, the woman who is building the casino, she loves the title. The Karuk guy who is doing the videoing said it was like calling Indians niggers. We are stepping in a lot of shit with this, but I think that is very interesting. That is another aspect of reflecting the community back. Not as "this is the way it should be," but reflecting that conflict back.... I think we have agendas in that way, too, in terms of shaping this place in a way that we feel would be more conducive to more of that kind of back and forth.

So, in the mirroring of their community, Dell'Arte provides a place for conversation, for "back and forth," about matters people care about. The conversation is based on people the audience recognizes, feels familiar with, but the conversation carries with it values and conflicts we all typically duck, shy away from – fear of change, cross-cultural interactions, social mistakes and forbidden words that reveal prejudice and other human faults.

Something extraordinary begins to be apparent. These are the things a democracy implies, but with which people in a democracy have to contend in order to accomplish the mutual goals of living together. By making its theatrical creations, Dell'Arte has become a part of the democratic process of contention and resolution in Blue Lake. By careful artistic purpose, the theater that Dell'Arte makes is an expression of the human and social forces at play in their community.

The ensemble's careful self-awareness, their disciplined commitment to deep learning about the people and community with whom they live has resulted in their maturity and their clarity of vision. This is the base for their success and the source of the pride with which the citizens of Blue Lake claim them as their own.

Twenty-five years since their arrival in town, everyone can see that the Dell'Arte players had more than redwood-sized ambition, Paul Bunyan courage and an incredible amount of Pollyanna hope. As one of their fans, a guy named David who talked with the project interviewer at the Logger Bar in Blue Lake, said, "They are just damn good theater."

Charlene Sanders, a second-grade teacher, puts it another way, "One really nice thing about the community, too, is Dell'Arte kind of being the heart of Blue Lake." This is a strong metaphor. She's not saying that the theater is in the center of Blue Lake (though Dell'Arte is smack downtown). She says Dell'Arte is the heart of Blue Lake. For her, the theater actually expresses the inner feelings, the strongly held beliefs, the fears and dreams of the whole town in which she lives and works. Ron Brunson, retired post master and 30-year resident of Blue Lake, refers to Dell'Arte in the same terms. He says that without the theater, the town "would be deader. A lot deader. It may be totally dead." For the people of Blue Lake, Dell'Arte has become integral to who and how they understand themselves to be.

In a one-industry town, when that industry goes under, the fear of dying is real. Dell'Arte doesn't just tell jokes for small-minded reasons of making fun or getting a laugh. Dell'Arte uses its comedic skills to release unspoken truths, truths that the town knows but can't or doesn't say. This is heart's blood for a community. Commonly held truths, publicly acknowledged and celebrated, could be considered one of the basic elements of human community. To tell the truth and be heard, to remain consistent with the community's experience, even when revealing secrets is the function of good theater. The Dell'Arte Players and the citizens of Blue Lake understand this in very specific and real terms

Peter Pennekamp, a longtime fan of Dell'Arte and an executive of the Humboldt Area Foundation, identifies one specific example of astonishing import. Referring to one of Dell'Arte's plays, he says,

> "Korbel One" was the most powerful in part because it is about the decline of the paternalism of timber. ... I don't think anyone [had] actually articulated that the issue of timber decline wasn't just jobs, but a whole notion of being taken care of by an industry. That was the first time that had been raised. It was raised through drama in ways that were very emotional for people and went right to local politics. Very powerful stuff.

The public nature of revealing truths through a play is for Pennekamp the key ingredient. He says,

> That those issues got to be a part of public discourse meant that the way people saw the timber industry changed. ... Within about two years the timber industry had fallen off their perch. Totally different reactions. People saying that they had always known that we were fouling our nest, and that it is time that we took better care of things. Pacific Lumber was going so extreme that almost everyone abandoned any hope of supporting them. They were the model, that paternalistic model. So, the art and what was happening in the community coincided in a way that public perception changed."

Pennekamp points out that the public and the artists, all together as a whole, know that the truths that the Dell'Arte artists express in their plays come out of their community. The artists don't create the truth. They express it at a time and in a way that it can be heard. This, however, is no "simple" coinci-

---

The Dell'Arte Company

Location: Blue Lake, California (pop. 1,200)

Ensemble members: 18

Founded: 1977

Major activities: Creation of new work; Dell'Arte International School of Physical Theatre (full-time one-year program, summer workshops, and an MFA program in Ensemble-Based Physical Theatre; Mad River Festival; Education Through Art; touring of repertory;

Facility: Owns 114-seat theater, an outdoor amphitheater seating 350, two large teaching studios, offices, a guest artist apartment and small shop. Rents additional shop space, studio space, library space for school.

Annual budget: $1.2 million

Community Partnerships: Humboldt Folklife Festival, Blue Lake Elementary School, CenterArts of Humboldt State University, local food co-op and Credit Union, Institute of Native American Knowledge; Potowat Health Village, Tu Casa Center

Website: www.dellarte.com

Company Statement

Dell'Arte International is the United States center for the development, exploration, training, creation, and performance of the physical theater traditions and their contemporary applications. We are a true "regional" arts center for our geographically diverse community. We work in partnership with many local organizations and government agencies, and our combination of tuition, box office, tour income and foundation support generates well over a million dollars each year for the Humboldt County economy. Dell'Arte co-founder, Carlo Mazzone-Clementi, was a native of Italy and chose the name "dell'arte" (dell are tay) because it means "of the art." His work was inspired by the lively commedia dell'arte, a character -based style that has fueled popular theater for generations, and was known as "the art of the professionals." The combination of our training programs , research, our original touring productions, our education program in the public schools, our summer festival and our work in economic/community development make us a destination unlike any other on the American theater map.

---

dence. It is the result of years and years of the artists' commitment to the town, the whole community, as well as to their craft of theater making. The makers of the plays heard the truths in their research, as they listened to people in their town, their region. Over time, they built a trust that allowed people to talk with them, to share private thoughts. The skills of the players allowed these truths to be heard for the first time in a public way. This, then, can be understood as the point of theatrical skill and one of the essential hallmarks of good theater.

This specific comprehension of a relationship between the artists and the community exists with equal clarity on both sides of the equation. Jim, an audience member interviewed by this project, says Dell'Arte has become

> ... one of the pillars of the community now, not only because they are good artists. I think that is secondary. They have become that because they are good people. The plays are built on local issues, they treated all sides. In theater you need conflict. In community, if you are going to represent conflict, you have to treat all sides of the conflict with honor, dignity, and careful thought, which is rare these days. That is another thing I want to say. The principals have really tried to be fair in their presentation. I think they are harder on their own than on anybody else. That is the way you have to be. The community really respects that. In 20 years, it has turned around 180 degrees. No doubt.

In this thought Jim makes a leap, connecting "good people" traits to good theatrical practices. It is a leap that might be the envy of the professional critic, because the critic so rarely gets a chance to know the artists the way Jim and the rest of Blue Lake know the Dell'Arte players. Jim's praise, nevertheless, reveals a requirement of fairness, honor, dignity and careful thought that is a critical standard commonly held by many of those interviewed in this project.

Confirming Dell'Arte's intimate relationship with Blue Lake, Gene Supka, the proprietor of the Logger Bar down the street from Dell'Arte's theater, recognizes that the value of their plays lies in the fact that the audience from Blue Lake "knows the secrets behind the laughter." Supka's imagery reaches into the substance of the comedic form itself. To put the secrets of a community into the public forum and allow laughter to be shared by all, fairly and with respect, is the very essence of good comedy. It is this capacity to allow laughter and tears to spring from hidden secrets brought public that the ancient Greeks recognized as the healing power of the art. The comedians and philosophers of antiquity, so revered by scholars and critics, would share a grin of recognition with Blue Lake's barkeep.

This success has been achieved by great hard work on all sides. People in town tell stories of encounters between Dell'Arte actors and townspeople that reflect amazing cultural adjustments – personal, communal and economic all in the same breath. Pennekamp highlights the reality that the economic changes occurring out of Dell'Arte's presence and productions have come with cultural and social changes that affect everyone just as much.

People recognize and appreciate that these changes require specific sensitivity and effort from the ensemble. Person after person praises the company for finding the balance between speaking truth and not alienating segments of the community. They are proud that Dell'Arte models characters in their plays after specific people in the community, in part because Dell'Arte openly acknowledges those sources. Of course, the performers are also extremely deft in the execution of their art. Much to their local credit, Dell'Arte is known to have even asked community members to play themselves in certain shows. In one particular case, two women, each prominent activists but on opposite sides of the timber/environmental issues sang the duet "Anything You Can Do I Can Do Better," with rewritten lyrics around local political topics. The public moment was recognized and remembered throughout town – two people from hostile political perspectives working together. The performance allowed the town to reconsider established alliances and conventional perspectives.

Their honesty and integrity, combined with highly trained artistic skills, produces a form of theater that Dell'Arte's audiences recognize as powerful. People in Blue Lake describe this power in terms of the supernatural. When astonished beyond comprehension people have always attributed that to unknown forces. The magic of the Dell'Arte Company – the public revelation of privately hidden human truths, demystification of local secrets, transformation of commonly held perceptions, laughter in the face of communal struggle, the infusion of joy in the environment of fear, building healthy community through lasting partnerships – this magic is the result of well-tried practice.

In fact, the Dell'Arte Company is a treasurehouse of resources for those who would like to do similar work in their own communities. First, of course, is Dell'Arte's own training program through their school, the Dell'Arte International School of Physical Theater. Their international reputation and the constantly high level of excellence in their students is testimony to the quality of this educational institution. Beyond or aside from their formal training programs, the passion and commitment of the ensemble members is such that they are interested and willing to offer themselves and the documentation of their history as resources for those of similar mind. Their expertise extends to all aspects of the artistic enterprise.

The ensemble is more than open to inquiries, internships and other forms of sharing. What they have learned over their long history, the senior ensemble members teach in their school. The students work in the community as part of their training. A week's curriculum is balanced with serving food at the Grange's free Sunday breakfast program and other similar community-service programs around town. The students are taught that they can relate with their community in many ways, not simply as actors. Dell'Arte's understanding about how to relate could breathe life into dreary green rooms in theaters all across the country.

Marya Errin Jones, a former student in the school, states that flexibility is one of the things she has learned working with Dell'Arte. She describes flexibility as "trying to get a hold onto your own ideas, and claiming them whether they are right or wrong. Fighting for them. Not fighting each other, but fighting for the idea." It is remarkable that flexibility in this school for physical theater, with all its muscle stretching and body bending, is a concept of vision and cooperation, a principle for the development of plays through a group process. The artistic skills and craft that are taught in the school are the very practices that have welded the Dell'Arte Company into a durable and fertile ensemble. Daniel Stein, director of the School, teaches certain permanent principles that describe exactly what the ensemble members do every day, and have done since they first began their company: Be available to what was happening, in the now. See and hear and respond with honesty. Apply the lessons of good art making to the practice of good citizenship.

A significant portion of Dell'Arte's regular work involves art-in-the-schools programming. Their philosophy of long-term commitment and constancy makes their work stand out to teachers, children, parents and outside observers alike. Senior members of the ensemble teach in the schools. Furthermore, the same members of the ensemble are the in-school instructors for six or eight years running, without a turnover. This is quite unusual, compared to most artists-in-schools programs where new young artists travel through classrooms on single-appearance schedules, used all too often as short-term career stepping stones rather than long-term commitments to children, school and community. The Dell'Arte ensemble artists talk regularly with Blue Lake teachers about the school curriculum. They integrate their in-class theater projects with the teachers' needs. They have developed a deep professional relationship – a "conversation," to use Michael Fields' apt word, of real significance. Children recognize the value of working with artists who know them, who can build on the children's own assets and who can draw out new skills from students they work with over time. Parents view the Dell'Arte ensemble artist in the schools as an important adult figure beyond the usual mix of parents and teachers. The children know the artists around town, outside of school, as adults who will speak with children from a place of shared experience, shared knowledge.

Consistent with their theatrical approach, Dell'Arte's administration is rooted in collective collaboration. There was a time when everyone did everything at Dell'Arte. That time has passed. The organization has become more layered as it has become larger, more successful. That story is an exploration of how power can be shared amongst people with common intent and differing capabilities. The company has become good at this careful yet effective style. The structure of the organization is based on what the ensemble members call the "Hub." This structure defines how power is shared through several specific people, emanating outwards to include all who associate with the organization.

Many ensemble companies use this form, each one uniquely defined by the immediate realities of the people and community involved. At Dell'Arte, the seven members of the Hub elect the company's board of directors, which only meets once a year. In response to this project's survey, the company states: "Abandonment of traditional board of directors reflects locale and the fact that staff ended up doing everything anyway." Michael Fields astutely points out that when the organizational structure is not "normal," not what people are used to, it is important to make the structure especially apparent and available.

> I think in ensemble theater, in particular, it is easy to get stuck in both individual patterns of relating to each other and holding on to history and letting that determine current practice. Both of those things are dangerous. Because [Dell'Arte] has gotten larger there has been also an influx of new people working here who don't understand naturally the history and the kind of jargon of those who carried it around. So we needed to make the structure more transparent, more clear to people. How things work.

This is the kind of conscientious sharing that has made Fields known to be easy to work with, open to try anything and a willing partner. The overarching principle of this kind of structure is nonhierarchical power distribution, while acknowledging and utilizing the function of leadership within the organization. Joan Schirle talks about the nature of this in terms of a careful mix of removing ego from compromise and removing compromise from vision. She equates her vocational discipline with religious vows.

> How do you be in and of the world, and of your time and of your field, and still hold to these ideals [of collaborative, ensemble process] that are practically monastic in a way? If you take them that seriously, they are. There are the orders of people who usually band together around religious ideas or strong political movements. I don't think we take our-

selves that seriously, but, if you look at things, there is that.

The personal disciplines implied in their art work and their school work, as well as in Dell'Arte's organizational and structural strength and flexibility are the result of growth over many years. Whether touted for their magical accomplishments or their monastic disciplines or their cooperative collaborations, the Dell'Arte Players provide us with a rich expression of damn good theater.

An excerpt from "Korbel" (First Episode: The Funeral)

By the Dell'Arte Company

© 1993, M. Fields, D. Forrest, J. Schirle, J. Weisman. All rights reserved.

The "Korbel" series was created by the company over several years and is a kind of Humboldt County soap opera with recurring characters. The themes mirror the changes happening in the area once known for logging and fishing, now a depressed economy increasingly dependent on tourism and dwindling resources. The Dugan family of Korbel, a small mill town, are the central figures for whom change is painful and threatening. Dorothy (Dot) Dugan and her two sons, Terry and Tommy, are descended from the town's founders, but are barely managing to stay solvent. At the beginning of "Korbel" (The Funeral), the mayor, members of the family, and mourners stand around the casket of Dorothy, who died under suspicious circumstances. As the funeral goes on, her son Terry, a Vietnam vet who now dresses as a woman, is accused of murdering his mother. At the height of the accusations, the coffin springs open and Dorothy arises to declare her son innocent. In a series of flashbacks, she tells of the events leading up to her death. In this scene, Tommy has been laid off from the mill, and has just accused his brother of being responsible for their family setbacks and threatens to reveal Terry's secret identity.

DOT:

Don't you think your brother is suffering enough? Don't you think we'd all suffer if anyone was to find out? Don't you know we got to pull together here?

TOMMY:

I can't take it much longer, Ma.

DOT:

I don't want to hear any quitter talk.

TOMMY:

Ma, don't you get it? Nothin's like it used to be.

DOT:

You mean you haven't got any guts no more.

TOMMY:

According to you, Ma, I never had no guts. It was always Terry who had the guts and the glory. What you never did do was treat me like I was a equal.

DOT:

What I didn't do was smack you enough to knock any sense into you. Now you're going to hold on. You're gonna hold on to your mouth until we figure out something for Terry. So maybe you're gonna have to hold on to your mouth till you die. You're gonna hold on until you go back to work, and you're gonna hold onto that girl you got into trouble and marry her and start another family and try to make something work out for once in your life. Heck, a layoff isn't the end of the world. You just wait it out. The mill's always taken care of you. Square your shoulders like your grandfather Martin would want to see you doin' and quit snivellin' around here like you was some welfare slacker.

TOMMY:

Aw, Ma. (pause) Yeah, I guess I could turn out some more of them ashtrays.

DOT:

Now that's the spirit.

VOICE OFFSTAGE OF WOODY, THE NEWSBOY:

Extra! Extra! Read all about it!

DOT OPENS DOOR.

WOODY:

"Mill closes for good! Hundreds lose jobs as Simpson moves to Chile!" (Hands Dot her paper) Hi, Mrs. Dugan. Pretty heavy news, huh? Can I collect for this month's paper?

DOT:

Give Woody the paper money, Tommy.

TOMMY:

I ain't got it, Ma.

DOT (brightly):

Tell you what, Woody, why don't you come back on Thursday, and we'll see you get your money then.

WOODY:

OK. But that'll be two months you owe me.

DOT:

You'll get your money Woody. You always do, don't you? (Shuts door)

TOMMY:

Aw, jeezus.

(He sits at table, starts to cry. Dot reads the paper, puts it down and starts to cry quietly.. Finally Tommy stands up. He gets a beer.)

DOT:

And that ain't gonna do you no good, neither.

TOMMY:

Aw, Ma, it's just a beer, fer chrissakes.

DOT:

Alright, well then, give me one too.

TOMMY:

Ma...!

DOT:

Well, it's kind of a red letter day, isn't? I have a feeling you boys are going to need something extra special for dinner. I got a venison casserole in the freezer. I'll just get it out and put it in the microwave and –

TOMMY: (Stands up)

(Quietly)I'm going down to the welfare office, Ma.

DOT:

Tommy!

TOMMY:

I'm just gonna go ask some questions, find out what – There ain't no money coming and there ain't gonna be – What the hell's a man gonna do?? I'm whipped, Ma. It feels like – between them owls and them politicians – we're getting pushed right off the edge.

DOT:

But not into despair, Tommy.

TOMMY:

We're in deep poop, Ma. How we going to eat? How'm I gonna

pay my goddam child support? And Rhonda's got a list as long
as my arm of stuff I'm supposed to buy for her and that baby.

DOT:

What's your son Willie going to say? What's he going to think of
his daddy? I'll smack you upside your head if you think you're
going to bring free money into this house!

TOMMY:

We ain't even gonna have a house no more if I don't do this, Ma.
The house is all we got!

DOT:

We got our brains, don't we? We got our guts, don't we? We got
our values and our sweat and our pride, don't we? We got generations of hard work and honesty, don't we?

TOMMY:

We got squat, Ma. And nobody gives a shit. (He exits)

DOT:

And then he left and I said to myself, damn him, damn that little coward, that sonofa bitch! I started to get mad. I started to
get mad that my sons didn't have the strength to shoulder their
load and carry on with a smile. And I started to thinking about
my grandaddy Martin and what he woulda said. Well, that gave
me a shot of courage. I went to take the casserole out of the
freezer. It was dark in the freezer and the turkey next to the
casserole was kind of soft. I thought the fridge is just on the blink
again. I put the casserole into the microwave and turned it on.
Nothing happened. And then I walked over and turned on the
light. And nothing happened. And that's when I realized the
PG&E had shut off the electricity. I flipped the switch again.
Nothing happened. I stood there for a long time. I kept flipping
that switch, up and down up and down and up and down. And
I stood there, just absentminded-like, like an idiot, flippin' that

switch back and forth, up and down, waiting for the lights to come on. That's what we'd all worked for! I thought about my granddaddy. Heck, we'd all worked for it our whole lives – the right to just... flip a switch and have it all work. And I wanted it to be just like that again. I wanted to be able to flip that switch and have it all work. I wanted things to be the way they were. I wanted my microwave to cook that food! And then something snapped. And suddenly, I started to see red, and without thinking another thought about it, I ran out the back door to the shed and turned on the emergency generator. And I came back into the kitchen and I turned the lights on and off about one hundred times, and then I went and opened the door of the microwave, set the timer for 30 minutes, took a crochet hook, like Tommy taught me how to make a connection when the door was broken, and I stuck my head in the microwave and pressed the crochet hook into the door latch and pushed start with my other hand. There was a blinding light....

So don't any of you blame my baby boy. I did it myself. I just don't know why the pain didn't go away.

JUMP-START PERFORMANCE CO.: Magic Glue – The
Politics and Personality of Jump-Start
By Ann Kilkelly

JUMP-START PLAYWRIGHT DIANNE MONROE describes what holds Jump-Start Performance Co. together as "some kind of magic glue." It is an apt phrase, since magic involves sleight of hand, the illusion of effortlessness and transformation whereas glue suggests deliberate construction and craft. In Keith Hennessy's interviews, there emerges a sense of creative energy located in a powerful melange of individual artists, of conscious and talented leadership in managerial and artistic practices; and of a big commitment to sweat equity and fun. In its 17th year, exhibiting artistic vitality and a remarkable degree of fiscal health, Jump-Start has evolved as a significant grassroots organization. They have been able to "stick together" through flexible and evolving organizational structures and artistic processes that are both constructively critical and inclusive. The magic here is the sustenance of a wild energy and will to play, a belief in the individual imagination, and the practice of grounded political analysis.

Jump-Start's definition of community is very broad and inclusive, yet they work in extremely distinct communities and neighborhoods, building connections and long-term relationships. This remarkable assemblage of personalities and talents is itself a community of choice. They interview like they work, with practiced conversational and public reflection skills, and the accumulated intensity of the interviews is greatly enhanced by interviewer Keith Hennessy's like-mindedness with the Jump-Start company members and his reflections via his own work.

Hennessy's front statement, "A company needs money and a room of its own to create quality performance work," underscores the fundamentally political and economic nature of aesthetic judgments and organizational structures. Indeed, Executive Director Steve Bailey remarks, "To me, aesthetics are politics and politics are aesthetics." Jump-Start was founded to create and support new work by artists from underserved communities by helping individuals find voice and a space, including the public space of performance. As in so many grassroots organizations studied here, Jump-Start's strengths are precisely its challenges: operating within and outside of boundaries of arts funding, resisting or supporting dominant public ideology, finding a balance between advocacy and creative expression. As Hennessy writes:

> The performance and education work of Jump-Start not only serves but participates in several historically underserved communities, helping to birth and develop community identity, leadership and vision. Much wisdom and strength comes directly from the diversity of company members, who are deeply rooted in specific communities united by ethnicity, neighborhood, sexuality, art medium, political struggle, age, gender or collective vision. As a multicommunity, polycultural resource, Jump-Start is also the site and inspiration of cross-community collaborations, which honor specific cultural histories while engaged in the dangerous yet fertile practicing of cultural border crossing.

Jump-Start is an ensemble that doesn't look like other grassroots community organizations. In its more than 50 performances a year there are widely diverse performance styles – solo work, campy extravaganzas, local historical plays, musical ensemble pieces, and work by many well-established and younger writers and performers. They do not share a single performance methodology or leadership style, although the leadership is clear, because their intention is to have real diversity. They do have well-developed processes of self-critique and long-term partnership building. With characteristic hip political energy, they notice and respond to where they are, literally and metaphorically.

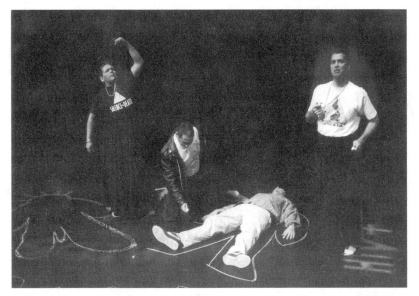

"Quinceanera", Left to right: Michael Marinez, Beto Araiza, Paul Bonin-Rodriguez
Photo credit: Edward Cohen

Artistic Director Sterling Houston says, "The easiest way to explain that is that it becomes a company piece when it is created by a company member." The "generator" of the piece may or may not actually use the company performers in an individual piece, but the company will support and commit to realizing the vision. Jump-Start has made work that draws material from the gay/lesbian/bi communities, African-American communities, Chicano communities and women, yet the work comes originally from an individual whose passion reaches out in specific ways. The diversity of the company generates diverse work. This allows individual artists to bring a variety of political perspectives to the group by way of the creative work.

Borders and Audiences

A literal kind of border-crossing, from one neighborhood to another, or from one clear community group to another, is often a part of progressive cultural work. In a "liberal" model, an organization strives to bring the underserved into the allegedly "served" or mainstream community, stressing opportunity, representation and inclusion. "Radical" or "alternative" work, on the other hand, stresses the marginalized or oppressed community by defining and validating core community identity. I think Jump-Start strategically uses both of the above models, but it also operates within the "material" structures of historical contexts and existing economic and social conditions. This results in work sometimes edgy and intellectual, sometimes accessible and celebratory; sometimes based on highly popular forms, sometimes abstract and experimental. Common ground comes in a deliberate and conscious conversation about the efficacy of the work, and in a strong group sense of speaking from the margins of many discourses and social arrangements.

Steve Bailey is impatient with unchallenged ideas of how borders are crossed, and the too frequent assumption that if people come to see a show about a particular community that they will necessarily be changed by it. Sounding like an artistic director and grant writer who has often been called on to connect the number of audience members to "impact," he comments:

> It is also about this crossover audience bullshit. Crossing communities. So we get a gay male audience for this, we get a black audience for this. Fuck it. Fine. I'm tired of thinking that it is our responsibility to get these gay men to come and see this black show and to make sure these black folks come to see this gay show. It's not going to happen, and I'm not worried about it anymore. We know that we have a certain core audience that will cross over. Usually straight white women that will come see anything that we do. There are others that are resistant. We can't break – that is society. We are there to push a few bricks off that wall, but we can't make that wall tumble down. You can get a little peephole here and there.

Bailey's wall metaphor is consistent with Jump-Start's realpolitik – tumble a brick, make a peep hole – get vision and deconstruction a little at a time. And he understands that change is long-term and slow, and involves going to the community more than bringing audiences in. "Cross-over" may be a totalizing term, insisting on separation, or borders that a dominant culture needs to keep intact. Bailey's remarks imply, on the other hand, that learning and change are probably not the amalgamation of audiences at a theater, but in schools and curricula that build performances and long-term relationships with educators and children.

Spectators and Spectacle

In "The Feminist Spectator as Critic," Jill Dolan argues that the way we think about audiences is constructed and therefore also limited by the same arrangements that mark social institutions. She argues that feminist theater (or I would add queer theater or another kind of performance that is marginal to mainstream culture) requires taking apart many assumptions about how the concept of audience is constructed. Our imagination of audience, for example, is often monolithic, and if not monocultural, it at least assumes a virtue in unity, in the bringing together. By imagining that spectators can or should be in one audience and should all come, perhaps we are suggesting a monodirectional gaze of the performance itself.

Bailey underscores the difference between real impact on very small and specific audiences through sustained work, and the kind of proposed idealistic paradigm shift that is explicitly if not implicitly demanded by so much social-change work. It is neither successful nor desirable to imagine that the separate cultural identities of the groups will blend somehow into one joyous entity of the audience.

Sterling Houston, answers the question of impact differently, but with a similar sense of how the theater can shift or change thinking:

> People that might have been judgmental about our work and our politics are less so when they see the work we have done with education. ... That we are in the schools, that we are doing this really grassroots, nuts and bolts, academic

115

work with the curriculum, with the students, with the teachers and producing over a period of years. It is like, well, maybe all the things I heard about queers aren't true. I've almost had people say that to me. "I thought it was this way. My husband told me that you guys had this agenda and you don't." I think that has become a practical outcome, it is one of the realities.

Many other pieces produced by the organization, past and present, are deliberately edgy, especially as they "cross over" in unexpected ways. I think that the ability to address what children need in schools without the overlay of a particular politics is balanced with the radicality of work often produced in the theater.

Houston's description of his early work with the company offers a glimpse of the importance of satire and humor in the work he makes for the company and the community.

Because of my background and my racial and sexual orientation, I have a certain view of conventional history that really affects how I interpret it and how theatrically it is presented. I would never think of myself as a gay writer or a black writer, but certainly my being gay and being black totally affect the way my work is presented and envisioned. That is tough for some people. It is like splitting hairs. But it isn't for me, it is very clear.

The first play we did together was called "Womandango," which was this race-and-sex-reversed piece set in Antebellum South that really satirized black stereotypes that are used in film. It was many things, but that is basically what it was. It wasn't about slavery, but it had slavery in it. It had whites playing the slaves, and blacks playing the masters, and women playing the men. It sounds like a handful, but it was quite accessible after five minutes of you being shocked. Then you just accepted it because the roles are so defined and the clichés were explored so thoroughly. That was a success. It won a national award. We went to Chicago and we did it in Chicago. It was a disaster. The press hated it. The black intellectuals wanted to string me up. They didn't see beyond the six-foot-tall black man in a pink hoop skirt.

Jump-Start Performance Co.

Location: San Antonio, Texas (pop. 1,150,000)

Ensemble members: 20

Founded: 1985

Major activities: Creation of new work; presenting; international Festival de Libre Enganche; Young Tongues festival; Works In Progress performance series; children's Shakespeare festival; Healing Arts program; arts-in-education program, visual art gallery

Facility: Rents office and theater space in Blue Star Arts Complex in inner-city San Antonio.

Annual budget: $300,000

Community Partnerships: Esperanza Center; Guadalupe Cultural Arts Center; Carver Community Cultural Center; Centro Cultural Aztlan; Burras Finas Productions; San Antonio Theatre Coalition; Cultural Alliance of San Antonio; madmedia; Zona Libre; Dance Umbrella; Kelly, Bonham, Hawthorne, Douglass and Japhet Elementary Schools; Poe and Dwight Middle Schools; Memorial and Tejeda High Schools; Westside Boys and Girls Club; Say Si; Gemini Ink; Alamo Children's Advocacy Center's CARE Project

Website: www.jump-start.org

Company Statement

Jump-Start Performance Co. is a group of diverse artists dedicated to the discovery and the support of new ideas in performance. By encouraging visionary thought and non-traditional approaches, Jump-Start Performance Co. is committed to the creation of art that is a lasting voice of many diverse cultures.

Man of color in a big pink dress. They couldn't see the ideas beyond that. They stopped right there. Paul Carter Harrison, who is a black intellectual playwright and theorist, said that I had set back black theater by 50 years. Things that you just don't forget.

School Programs

In 1991, Jump-Start created Historias y Cuentas in a number of public schools, and since that time, Houston remarks that in some schools they have worked with kids from third grade to graduation. They have cultivated programs with schools in their own neighborhoods. Teachers speak with deep enthusiasm about what Jump-Start has given, about their artistry and their warmth, and, tellingly, the company members speak about what they have learned. Their education projects involve training for the teachers and for the theater artists, conversations about how kids learn, training about challenges children might be facing, and explorations about what kinds of materials art projects can use successfully. In practical ways, Jump-Start artists have learned not to assume that their status as artists specifically equips them for the work of community exchange. Rather, they seek training and work with partner artists and educators to sustain community work. Alva Ibarra, principal at Kelly Elementary School, describes the affection and depth of Jump-Start's relationship with her school:

> They are part of our family now here at Kelly. The kids see them and they know them. We want that. We want them to be able to just come in here. They are part of our staff. Everybody accepts them and we are just happy to have them here.

Finally, Ibarra and other teachers and school administrators have come to understand and appreciate that art making involves very specific skills, and that those skills have an important place in the education of young people. Bailey's notion of exchange is born out in the long-term hard work of these residencies

The Festival de Libra Enganche, the Young Tongues Program and the Healing Arts Program, as their names suggest, reach out to particular communities, bring in the voices of artists around the country, and focus on particular issues or community needs.

Their work in education tends to be about the foundational process of using the imagination rather than about transmitting a particular cultural analysis, although the analysis may be operating on a tacit level. This foundational work, I believe, is the first level of advocacy, because it locates power, or inspiration, in the process of art making, which is individual, collaborative, and public.

Alva Ibarra describes a school project at Kelly that typifies how these partnerships work:

> Last week, they (the children) did the city council. I thought it was great. These kids were wonderful. We had our little mayor, Mayor Kelly. And they reenacted the way the city council runs their meetings. We even had some kids picking up erasers and talking on the phones while the meeting was going on. I really enjoyed that; I got a kick out of that part. They were doing a persuasive piece: why they should have a park, and other citizens were saying why they shouldn't have a park. This fits perfectly into what we are doing.

Work in education has become increasingly important in Jump-Start's focus and time investment. Bailey says he is really "jazzed" about education work, and there is a sense that this shift takes time and energy that might have previously been spent in creating ensemble performances. Jobs in schools are important sources of income and clearly in line with the mission, but they do require huge amounts of time in planning, teaching, and assessing.

Solo Performance Work

Jump-Start has encouraged new writing and solo performance work that is extremely diverse. An analysis of the aesthetics and politics of a few pieces illustrates Jump-Start's community orientation in less obvious ways than the education and large ensemble and festival projects.

S.T. Shimi's "Southern Discomfort," for example, explicitly blends a harsh critique of all religion with stories of Shimi's young life as a woman of color who was born in Singapore of Indian parents and educated in New England in a conservative Christian church. She weaves her text with Middle Eastern belly dancing, a form which explicitly celebrates and exposes female sexuality. The shock of seeing an enactment of sexual identity in a culture not "her own" but easily conflated with hers via racial stereotyping is certainly the visual foreground, but the text also offers a feminist critique of religion, specifically Christianity, that

119

"tried to drive the devil out of me. They drove out God instead." "Southern Discomfort" is designed to produce just that. She deliberately messes with the stereotypical, and gendered/racialized identity, giving the lie to monocultural identity.

Dianne Monroe's "Comfort," offered in production with Shimi's piece, historicizes a moment of cultural resistance from a history that is not part of her particular identity but which clearly relates to her present politics and the complex dynamics of San Antonio's cultures. Monroe's piece is based on a moment in the history of Comfort, Texas, when a group of German immigrants who were Freethinkers, resisted slavery. Hennessy saw both performances during his visit and offers a cogent commentary on them. Among those interviewed after the show were people involved in developing the Comfort piece. Most interesting were interviews with teen audience members and volunteers who obviously had never seen anything like either of the pieces, but who were clearly intrigued and open to Shimi's probing of religion and Monroe's presentation of antislavery commitment in a remote historical period.

Paul Bonin-Rodriguez's work has similar qualities. "Memory's Caretaker," as I saw it performed at the FOCAS meeting in Lexington, Kentucky, in May 2002, politically connects the deeply private and intimate experience of care-giving and -taking with the isolation and conflicts of several cultural identities. Bonin-Rodriguez embodies and queries many identities: as a young gay man, an assimilated Chicano, a member of a dysfunctional Southern Christian family, an artist and a caregiver.

The performance's gestural phrasing suggests the invisible and the visible, working movement phrases that evoke the presence of the (now dead) grandmother in the present moment. Memory and politics ghost each other. The effect is moving, humorous and analytical in its use of feminist perspectives, queer theory and multiple visible and invisible racial and ethnic identification.

Bailey's direction enhances the complexity of the pieces, just as Jump-Start leadership combines open acceptance and encouragement with pointed political analysis of its art and its organizational practices. Bailey's articulation of his own role expresses the coherence of politics and practice:

> I know what I am feeling artistically what is really helpful for me is that I've quit using the term "director." I feel a strength of mine is to help people do their best work. I know I implant my artistry on it, too, but I feel like I have a talent with helping artists.

What matters here is a dynamic that I see repeated between and among many Jump-Start artists – the understanding that "helping" is an artistic function that involves making one's expertise available to another without seeking control or its own vision.

Process and Parties

Helping make others' visions manifest is a mode of operation that insures conversation. The conversation becomes a fertile ground for ideas, which, as Lisa Suarez describes, just "pop up."

> I think that the ideas come from some cosmic being that we don't know about that visits us in the middle of the night when we are dreaming. I think it visits every company member for some reason. It is not so crazy to talk about things like that here. It happens and they pop up in meetings. They pop up over lunch. They pop up at social gatherings when we are partying and that kind of thing. We come back and regroup and ask each other, "Were you serious about that idea?" Some things happen really fast, and other things you think about over a month or even over years before they actualize. I think that if you are working here and you are a company member, you certainly have the forum to dream and envision. If you have the guts and you are ready to take the risk, this is a place where you can do it. Got a plan? Let's work at it and see what we can do.

The mysterious, the "cosmic" of dreams notably requires guts and risk and hard work. Again, magic glue.

Shimi says, "Our passion is formal, but how we celebrate it is not," marking the combination of tremendously open and flexible social and organizational structures with the practiced and rigorous formalities of making performance. A great example is Jump-Start's performance parties, a yearly celebratory event that is a marathon of work, both curated and wide open, as Houston describes it. WIP or Wednesdays in Performance is also cited as a blend of the social and the formal, coordinated by Shimi. A wonderful exchange between Houston and Bailey describes the pride and chagrin and overwhelming sense of community at the events:

> SH: If something sucks, well, it only sucks for five minutes and it is over. Then the next thing will not suck. It is like this whole thing.

> SB: And it is free. It is for our anniversary. Last year we had literally 800 people come. ... We probably have 4-500 people in the theater . There were only 200 seats and everyone else was along the wall, sitting along the stage, sitting in the wings ...

> SH: It is a social event.

> SH: As an audience member and as a lover of performance and seeing it, I have had some of my highest moments at performance parties. My jaw just has dropped. This gorgeous juxtaposition seeing a little boy with Downs Syndrome dancing to the salsa group. I lost it. He was so happy, and we were, too. It's the moments like that that only happen at performance party, because it has such an open door.

> SB: So democratic. And the next moment your head is in your shirt.

> SH: Or you leave the room

Leadership

Many joke about the sign on the wall that says, "Be careful what you ask for" because you will probably find yourself doing it. Lisa Suarez describes "meetings, meetings, meetings" and an action cited by more than one person – Steve Bailey pulling out the calendar. There is both opportunity and challenge in this moment, a belief in potential and practice and the best learning ground. And resources go to the project, resources that include the collective labor of the group and the mechanisms of the organization. Repeatedly company members describe getting a start at something they always wanted to do and finding resources and encouragement in the group.

Jump-Start uses Liz Lerman's "critical response process" so skillfully that several members have become facilitators of the process. They use it in their meetings and retreats and following their own productions.

Leadership is not accidental or by default. Virtually all members, when asked, rather wryly but clearly say that Steve Bailey is the core leader, much the way Carpetbag members indicate Linda Parris-Bailey's leadership. There is also shared responsibility arrived at in difficult and frequent group processes, their annual retreat and a great deal of conscious processing. A signal moment in the interviews describes a turning point in the organization and a difficult leadership decision:

An exchange between Bailey and Hennessy contains some of the most important insights to emerge from these pages, as the two pinpoint an organizational crux that challenges so many groups trying to have democratic procedures and nonhierarchical structures where power distribution is damaging or limiting.

> SB. I'll never forget that you did that thing about, "Oh, I hate having to be the one to do this – " and you called me and said that I needed to own my leadership. Don't deny it, just because you feel like there is some kind of power inequity. Sometimes leadership is the way to give people more power not less power. It is the difference between tyranny and leadership.

> KH: The tyranny of structurelessness is where you refuse to create structure because it is based on the assumption that structure is inherently unfair or patriarchal. What you notice is that in the lack of structure it is very easy for cer-

tain people to take advantage of it. And then you will also notice that they maintain the structurelessness because it gives them power. One of the things that I see at Jump-Start is that there is a dare to actually make a structure. There is staff, there are resources, there is space, you have to maintain a building. These things you can't pull off if you are all equal all the time. You wouldn't have gotten there. Within that structure, it is built-in that there is inclusivity, an openness, a constant drive to find new voices.

Company members report having voice and the oppportunity to argue and be listened to by others. They operate on consensus, but when a tough decision needs to be made, Bailey makes it, usually with the close participation of Sterling Houston. It is remarkable that most company members not only describe being part of decision making, but that they can see the leadership process in others, in the visible struggles with issues and practices.

Again Suarez gives a good picture of the dynamic of shared power within a clear structure:

> It is kind of like Steve, and then the rest of us are all associate directors. There is not anything really below it other than our interns. I'll tell you, though, that I make the decisions on most of the things that I have to deal with. We've learned to be very strong. I've learned to put my foot down and say, "I don't agree with you Steve." He'll listen, he may not always like it. I love that man. I really, really do. I butt heads with him like you would not believe. We've cried together. We've pointed things out to each other, like when I feel like he has been racist or sexist in some ways or whatever. He will take it and apologize afterwards.

A final very revealing example of this combination of participation and visible leadership is the decision, widely discussed and definitively presented by Bailey and Houston, was to declare that new members of the company would be people of color.

SB: You know what I am thinking about, don't you?

SH: That board meeting? ...

SH: It was new members. It was new company members. Steve made the "outlandish" statement that, yes, we were going to get new members to the company, but they had to be people of color. Because we had enough white people. People of color bring something to the mix that white people can never bring, and that is the experience of having lived in that skin. What that can do to make the whole company more resonate and more full, the vision more complete. All the usual comments were made like: "No, we just have to bring the most talented person in. What if the most talented person happens to be white?" Steve says, well, we won't bring them in. It was shocking. I thought they were going to kill him, or all just walk out. No one walked out. ... Of course, the people of color that came into the company, it did make a big difference. In a way it was symbolic. It changed the whole company. Nobody is typically Mexican, or typically black. That is a myth. My work never fit with any black company at all. It fit more with Jump-Start, because it was so wide open. It fit what I wanted to do.

SB: I don't think I was conscious of this, but I knew I had power with these white people, if they followed me, to do my work. I had the power to change and make the company as I believed was right. If that wasn't acceptable to them, I was willing to accept the consequences of one of them leaving. One of the wonders of Jump-Start is there are several members who I really feel have grown through the process. Now, I don't think they have changed, radically changed politically, but I really think they get that idea that was brought up then that certain people because of their background can bring certain resources to you that you can't just because you don't have that background. Just that kind of basic principle that diversity is part of talent. It is part of nature, and what we do.

A Sense of Beauty

In his conversation with Hennessy, Bailey talks about his excitement for visual design, and about his own evolution as an artist and political thinker. Talks about having this sense of beauty, of a return to art making as infused and necessary, rather than direct action:

> That is kind of my style. I really like, I mean I am not shy about aesthetic values. I love to see work that is gritty, edgy, dirty. Those works send me through the roof, but that is not the work I do. For me, I really have this ... I like this sense of beauty.

It seems deeply important that this sense of beauty is infused with the pleasure of spectacle. This quality marks much of the work I have seen of Jump-Start's, no matter how diverse the style or subject whether the medium is visual imagery, words, movement or music. The pleasure seems connected to the space and time dedicated to talking about the work. A sense of the efficacy of the beautiful and the pleasurable underlies the politics, not the other way around.

Challenges

Jump-Start is growing and evolving in multiple directions. Like all the ensembles, they face the constant issue of funding and of their place in local and state arts funding. They have been deeply involved with arts politics in San Antonio, especially in their fight with the Esperanza Peace and Justice Center over that company's defunding because of rampant and organized homophobia. In this regard, as in others, their diverse income base is a strength, as is the employment artists find in school programs. The struggle is not only to survive, but also to continue to find time to create. As I write this, artists Monroe and Bonin-Rodriguez have left the company to concentrate on writing and performing their own work. The crux is how the ensemble creates as an ensemble, and will continue to develop. Shimi describes it this way:

> There are some things about how we work that are great. I

don't want to ever charge for a performance party. I don't want to ever do it two nights in a row. I want us to have dance at the theater. I'm still going to try and make a festival happen one day. There are some things I don't want to leave behind because it makes more sense for us to do opera or something. I think that is a constant challenge, but a good one. As long as we are always thinking about what Jump-Start means to us and what we want it to be then it will always be a fun place to hang your hat.

I like these words because they convey how much glue is evident in the willingness to acknowledge the truth of the present situation, a willingness to move on, an openness to change and a sense of value that comes from experience.

I'll conclude with one of Hennessy's best interview moments, where he poses this question to Suarez:

KH: If there is a way that you would want to leave a snapshot about what Jump-Start is, especially for someone who isn't from San Antonio or doesn't know what Jump-Start is, what do you want them to know? Or what do you want them to know about what is possible in terms of creating a grassroots theater company in their own place?

LS: Off the bat I was thinking this big old giant ANYTHING. Draw a sign on the wall. Sure, I mean there is anything, if you are willing to work at it and do it you can do it here. We've left it open to just about anything. If you believe in it.

An Excerpt from "Le Griffon," a tale of supernatural love

By Sterling Houston ©2000

Place: New Orleans, Louisiana

Time: 1803-10

PROLOGUE

(Music under. Lights up on Saint Louis Cemetery. During the following monologue, a funeral takes place. A small group of mourners weep and then move away slowly as FRANCOIS and PAULETTE creep into the scene. TANTE Honoree appears. She addresses the audience.)

TANTE:

I'm good and dead now, if dead be good. I seen everything before I died away. Even the dead who walk again. But I ain't no living dead. No, no. This ain't my old body you see before you now, but something lighter than the flesh. In my condition, I can only say what I know to be true. Got no reason to do otherwise. I was born not far from here in April of 17 hundred and 40. Nobody wrote down the day since in those times my mother was bonded to the house of Monsieur Jean-Pierre Treme. My papa, to tell the truth as I must, was a freeman and a fool. At 12 I was sold into the house of Monsieur August Le Favorite the undertaker. Monsieur trained me as a hairdresser for the dead ones. I got pretty good at my work and did it up till the time Monsieur died and freed me to go about my business. I bore 12 children, eight of them lived, one daughter was named Cecile. A bad luck name in truth, since she up and died after giving birth to her own daughter Paulette. Time passed. I raised up that child as best I could but the young Monsieur Julian Le Favorite, heir to his papa's fortune and trade, give Paulette as a gift to his son Francois. The two of them grew up together, thick as thieves. Francois and Paulette, came to this cemetery over and over, looking for fresh bodies to steal. They were doing dangerous work. Though it was necessary, it will no doubt end with both of them in hell. God help us. Some things must be done even if eternal damnation be the cost ...

(When the mourners are gone, FRANCOIS and PAULETTE approach a fresh crypt and remove the corpse. The hand of Jacob is 'highlighted' and removed from corpse by Francois. He crosses with it into lab area then begins to attach it to a prone body on slab. The body is obscured. Paulette crosses into lab area.)

SCENE 1

FRANCOIS:

All my life, I have been surrounded by death.

PAULETTE:

Yes, Francois.

FRANCOIS:

The son and grandson of undertakers does not posses the luxury of viewing death as a thing exotic ...

PAULETTE:

Yes, you are right, Francois.

FRANCOIS:

My first memory is that of watching my father work on the body of a little girl of five.

PAULETTE:

129

As you have said before ...

FRANCOIS:

Then came the deaths of my entire family when I was barely ten...

PAULETTE:

Oui, Cher; your dear maman, Marie-Louise, your granpere, your sister and both your little brothers dead of yellow fever within a month; may-their-souls-find-rest.

(PAULETTE lights candles and assists FRANCOIS.)

FRANCOIS:

I fear that death and I share an appalling intimacy.

PAULETTE:

No doubt, as you say, appalling indeed.

FRANCOIS:

What could possibly counterbalance such ill fortune?

PAULETTE:

Nothing could, Francois, but Monsieur must not forget that to die and thus fall into the everlasting arms of the Almighty is quite the only compensation for traversing this vale of tears.

FRANCOIS:

Dear Paulette, your faith in immortality is far greater than my own. (He finishes attaching the hand.) There. Help me move this away ...

PAULETTE:

Remember when you were a little boy and you would make little dolls and we would play with them. Remember? Sweet little dolls they were, out of rags and twine and horsehair. What a dear child you were then.

FRANCOIS:

I don't remember that.

PAULETTE:

Well it's true. Whether you admit it or not. You used to crawl into my bed with your doll and try to snuggle me. How marvelous.

FRANCOIS:

Help me put the blood back into him. (They begin business)

PAULETTE:

What wonderful doll have you made for us now?

FRANCOIS:

If only my father had lived to see him. And my grandfather.

PAULETTE:

Yes, cheri, they would be quite proud. They could only make the dead appear to be glamorously at rest, while you have resurrected Lazarus from the tomb. But he will be quite the harlequin man, no, sewn together like a patchwork. This will cause him much confusion, I suspect; seeing his one hand darkly brown and the other yellow-white?

FRANCOIS:

On the contrary. He will likely be clearer about these things than most. (Francois reveals the creature. He is both alluring and grotesque. Nude except for a loincloth, his stitches are visible and his eyes are closed.) Behold! The new man of the new century. (Lights fade)

LOS ANGELES POVERTY DEPARTMENT:
Theater as an Act of Citizenship
By Robert H. Leonard

THE LOS ANGELES POVERTY DEPARTMENT is a grassroots ensemble theater providing a forum and platform for community growth and participation among the homeless and very poor people located in the Skid Row district of Los Angeles. According to founder and artistic director John Malpede, who began the company back in 1985, its original goals were "to create community in Skid Row and get the voice of Skid Row out to the rest of Los Angeles and beyond." Malpede and his ensemble have spent the more than 15 years since doing exactly that – building community and getting the voice of the poor and homeless spoken, sometimes within Skid Row, sometimes as far beyond Skid Row as Cleveland and Chicago in the U.S. and Amsterdam and other cities of Europe. I am filled with awe for the artistic vision, the heroic determination and the practical know-how that undergirds this ensemble and its successes. I am also fearful that people will easily trivialize this ensemble simply because they are centered in a community that is, itself, marginalized and invisible to much of society. What does the Los Angeles Poverty Department do and what value does that have?

Malpede explains simply that "on one level the strategy is to make art." He goes on,

> It was a pretty extreme approach. I would cast [roles in the plays] to see who can grow [as opposed to who is stereotypically suited to the part], and to offer opportunities if

133

people wanted to expand. There are so many examples in 20th century art of breaking down the barriers between the professional and amateur. Everyone supports community-based art but it's [also] a code word for bad art. I felt like we were always fighting that. In many cases, we confounded those expectations by producing something that was undeniably good art.

Project interviewer Ferdinand Lewis describes LAPD's work as

gritty and artistically risky, often making powerful use of the contexts in which the pieces were performed. The work isn't crafted for charm, but rather to accurately reflect what Malpede calls "the wild energy of the neighborhood." There is no fixed artistic style for the ensemble, and, since he is simply trying to make the best art possible within a community context, Malpede has always allowed the material to decide the shape of the piece, rather than being guided by audience – or funder – expectations.

Workshops and community feedback sessions are integral to the production work of this company. Often material is developed through community workshops. Emmanuel Deleage describes how one show evolved during workshops intended to help abusers accomplish effective transitions during recovery. The material of the show was initially articulated and then rehearsed in the workshop environment. Lewis states in his field notes: "The aesthetic lines that separate theatrical and actual community interaction are intentionally and vigorously blurred. LAPD's research, development, and production style rely on an almost continual exchange of feedback with the community."

So, within Malpede's simple statement of a strategy to "make art," there is a virtual weather system of interchange, dialogue and inquiry in the community that surrounds the ensemble. Of course, as Lewis points out, "themes and subjects are always immediately [relevant] to the lives and experiences of Skid Row residents." He adds, "the ensemble's artistic approach has been primarily improvisational." The results are that the members' own experiences form the center of the art they make.

Video still from "Agents and Assets." Virgil Wilson as Mr. Dicks, Tony Parker as Mr. Bishop, Alexander Anderson as Mr. Lewis, photo credit: Lori Fontanes

In the case of "Agents and Assets," the show being performed at the time of these project interviews, LAPD's usual improvisational format was set aside for an entirely scripted piece. According to Lewis, the "script" was the literal transcript from a Congressional hearing on CIA involvement in crack cocaine sales in California. Lewis, who attended a performance, explains that

> long passages of dry, undramatic material were delivered by actors unused to either memorization or the delivery of such material. Text and context were clearly more important elements of the production than, say, performance technique. For the audience, it would have been difficult to overlook the irony of hearing the words of educated, skilled politicians spoken by actors who at some point in their lives were casualties of the Wars on Drugs. I spoke with audience members who were moved by the production, and they all agreed that it was the act of witnessing an event so fraught with contex-

tual weight that produced emotion in them, pathos for a plight, and not necessarily with the performer's character.

Malpede's stated goal of getting the voice of Skid Row out to the rest of Los Angeles and beyond was certainly achieved in the bitter irony Lewis describes.

The impulse to make art this way, to reach into the community surrounding the artist in order to create the ensemble and find material, leads inevitably to the formation of collaborative partnerships. However, in this case, the partnership building came first. Speaking of his own experiences starting LAPD, Malpede says,

> You have to be respectful of and take advantage of the resources that are there. I started [by] volunteering for activists and lawyers who were active in the community. I had to learn to be in that community, how to behave, and also learn the lay of the land. I kept redefining what was most important to me. Initially it was about helping out people who are already there. You have to keep your ear to the ground and be responsive to what's there. I think a lot of decisions are practical responses to what's in front of your face, trying to find the form for what's there.

Malpede also understands the time it takes to work this way. He recalls, "I was offered a job as a welfare advocate, I was hired by the Legal Aid Society of Los Angeles. ... We'd written a grant for workshops. ... I was going to make a piece about neighborhood issues. I started doing the workshops and it was a year before anything came out of it."

What value has this strategy? What consequence? On one level, the evidence offered in this study reveals that LAPD's long-term partnerships with other Skid Row organizations have resulted in overt change in the community. For example, when LAPD originally formed its partnership with SRO Housing Corporation "there were no SROs [single-room-occupancy hotels for the homeless] back then, they were all owned by private slum lords," says Malpede. "Now there are over 50 hotels [transformed out of old derelict buildings] that help Skid Row." LAPD and SRO Housing are pioneers in building this community.

On another level, LAPD itself has changed. No longer the greenhorn, at this juncture, LAPD has achieved a position to serve as a guide, an elder member of the community, helping new organizations find the lay of the land and learn how to behave to accomplish positive intentions. The adjustments, "acculturation" as Lewis calls it, required of newcomers to Skid Row can be learned by people who would do this work and, in turn, they can be taught to others. The relationship between LAPD and Side Street Projects, its partner for "Agents and Assets," outlines this mentoring function that LAPD provides.

Among the ensemble members, community partners and audience members that Lewis interviewed in this project, there are many perspectives and experiences, but all confirm LAPD's success in reaching its original goal of creating community through theater. Some refer directly to performances that were effective or moving for them. Others speak of how the success of LAPD has led to the creation of other organizations. LAPD is recognized as having inspired and/or assisted in the creation of several organizations, such as the Downtown Musicians Alliance and Artists In Recovery.

Ultimately, what LAPD makes, by way of product, is art that in itself, in the making of it and in the performing of it, creates, as Jeff Gilbert says, "culture and community and identity" where there was none recognized or claimed before. Organizations, people getting together to do something, whether to make plays or conduct workshops or just to learn from one another, are functional elements of community. The plight of the homeless, regardless of cause or circumstance, is the very absence of a sense of belonging and a sense of self-identity in the world. The interviews in this project attest to the abilities of this ensemble to accomplish what would seem to be the very deepest goals of our society: to create community where there was none, to create citizens where there were only survivors.

Tony Parker, a longtime ensemble member, speaks about his personal growth. He says, "It's helped me in terms of just relating to people. I used to be extremely introvert. ... But what this has done, it's braved me up in a lot of ways in terms of expressing myself."

Jeff Gilbert speaks of the transformative act of handing house keys to someone who has had no home. A similar transformation can and does happen when LAPD lets personal successes lead to leadership functions within the ensemble. Malpede's vision and expertise is knowing the importance of sharing organizational leadership tasks and being able to transfer those tasks successfully to those attracted to his ensemble.

So, how to reckon these successes? A woman named Denise H., a new member of the LAPD ensemble, makes one of the most startling observations in these interviews. About the ultimate value of publicly provided assistance she says, "You know these shelters and the recovery, the sobriety, stuff like that, that they have, but are they really, do they really care? What help are they giving? They aren't giving me any help. Now, I appreciate what they're doing but then to me personally, personally, my personal opinion on it is, it's to keep their foot on the top of me."

Denise H. is not the first person to come to this kind of conclusion, whatever its accuracy. Whole books and political careers have been built on the question of the difference between good-willed control of the poor and liberation of the poor. Nonetheless, Denise H. articulates her own tangible and immediate sense of the control of state agencies and programs.

Furthermore, Denise H. is finding her own voice, a voice she didn't know she had, by speaking in a public environment where other people, familiar to her, let her know she's been heard. The work of the LAPD has not simply been to offer Denise H. a role in a play. The LAPD, with its myriad partners, make it possible for Denise H. to formulate her own ideas about where she is living and how she would like to live with the other people in Skid Row.

LAPD's ensemble members make plays together, yes, but coming out of the creative process, they make their own organizations together. They identify their needs and develop their own agendas on how to satisfy those needs. In this realm, even if only for moments, they are no longer in the wicked loop of the dependent needy. For moments, the crushing brutality that exists in our society at the very bottom of the economic scale is being

Los Angeles Poverty Department

Location: Los Angeles, California (pop. 3,700,000)

Ensemble members: 17

Founded: 1985

Major activities: Creation of new work; workshops; Change/Exchange training institute; touring of repertory; commissions.

Facility: Borrows space in downtown Los Angeles from St. Vincent's Cardinal Manning Center and SRO Housing; rents rehearsal rooms at Los Angeles Theater Center.

Annual budget: $30,000-$100,000

Community Partnerships: SRO [Single-room Occupancy] Housing; L.A. Community Action Network; The Downtown Women's Action Coalition; St.Vincent DePaul Center; The Salvation Army's Women's and Men's drug recovery programs; and the Inner City Law Center.

Website: www.lapovertydept.org

Company Statement

LAPD's works to create challenging performances that express the realities, hopes and dreams of its group participants, people who live and work on Skid Row. The artistic purpose of the group is to create performance work that connects lived experience to the social forces that shape our lives and communities. LAPD's strives to make art that is a direct communication from its performers to its audiences and that is able to leap tall social barriers at a single bound. LAPD is dedicated to creating community on skid row and to the artistic and personal development of its members.

vanquished, not by give-aways but by the creative processes of making art. These moments are precious and valuable, for they hold the potential of breaking the cycle of dependency.

Ultimately, I think it is not possible to separate the impulse to make art, the very best possible, from the impulse to create culture, community and identity. I believe this is fundamentally true of all art. It is certainly and most consciously true of the art made by LAPD. I think the effort to separate these elements is destructive and ultimately cynical. The act of putting images of human behavior on stage for an audience to recognize and reflect upon is the act of theater. This act is intrinsically socio/political because the basic agreement between performance and audience, presentation and acceptance, spontaneously creates culture, community and identity. When theater is effective, this is what it does.

The theater artist who claims to shun the socio/political in favor of the so-called entertainment value of theater is simply denying these elemental aspects of the art. Likewise, the potential theater supporter, who claims a need to substantiate the capacity of good theater with quantitative data demonstrating evidence of social change in its audience, is at least in the same state of denial, if not willfully using false disciplines to avoid or deny support for excellent theatrical accomplishments. I know of no funding source that asks for quantitative evidence from our leading cultural institutions proving that audiences are more solidly entrenched in middle-class behavior patterns as a result of their participation in a given season of plays. In those circles it is simply assumed that good theater is good for its audience. The problem seems to come when the direction of change is not toward the mainstream status quo.

Project interviewer Ferdinand Lewis is driven by this same need to wrestle with the socio/political nature of theater when he observes that LAPD and other grassroots theaters do not

> necessarily have to effect measurable social change in order to be considered successful. In neighborhoods where most people have what they need to survive – and plenty of neighborhoods contain poverty yet fit that description – the change inspired by art may not have obvious political effect. ... Grassroots theater is not "medicine," but is first and foremost about making art to engage an audience (though that is in itself a sort of political act).

To create art, community and citizens, LAPD is a citizen first. From the very moment of its conception, LAPD has been invested in doing what needs to be done in the Skid Row district of Los Angeles. Through John Malpede's leadership, LAPD has partnered with social agencies, civic officials, arts groups and just about everyone who has a hand in the human endeavor of giving care to the needs of people in this most troubled part of the Los Angeles megalopolis. Like Michael Fields of The Dell'Arte

Company, John Malpede's history is one of being open to what others might need to do, how others might see value in the work of LAPD. This kind of artistic citizenship requires the kind of flexibility learned in the Dell'Arte International School of Physical Theatre by Marya Errin Jones, "trying to get a hold onto your own ideas, and claiming them whether they are right or wrong. Fighting for them. Not fighting each other, but fighting for the idea."

Referring to how these collaborations work, Emmanuel Deleage points out, "Any positive thing you bring in is welcomed. That's how you attract partners." These are fundamental rules of good ensemble practice. They are also fundamental for good citizenship. LAPD is both an ensemble and a citizen. Its art is a coherent, informed and moving expression of its community. There is no distinction between the artistic and the political, between art and social engagement. Art is political. Art is social engagement.

The value of this art lies in this connection.

An excerpt from "Agents and Assets"

By Los Angeles Poverty Department

[Note: This script is from the transcript of a Congressional hearing into allegations that the CIA was involved in selling drugs to the African-American community in Los Angeles to finance the Nicaraguan Contras. It was performed verbatim by the homeless and formerly homeless members of the Los Angeles Poverty Department. –Ed.]

THE CHAIRMAN (Mr Goss):

Mr Lewis.

MR LEWIS:

Thank you Mr Chairman and colleagues. Mr Hitz, I too appreciate your making the effort to come and be with us today and want to express my appreciation for your long service to the country. What were the CIA's legal and regulatory responsibilities from 1979 to '96 regarding the reporting of potential crimes and the maintenance of relationships with persons suspected of involvement in drug trafficking?

MR HITZ:

Well, it was a movable feast, so to speak, the requirements kept changing. From 1976 to 1982, it was an issue that was not really addressed. From 1982 to 1995, in an agreement hammered out between Attorney General Smith and the Reagan administration, there was no requirement to report on allegations of drug trafficking with respect to non employees of the intelligence agencies. And during the period that did not include agents of the CIA, did not include assets. That has been changed. The agreement in 1995 superseding the 1982 to 1995 period, specifically lists narcotics crimes as reportable, irrespective of whether or not the agency acquires information that they are being carried on by non-employees, namely assets.

MR LEWIS:

Thank you very much, Mr Hitz. Mr Chairman, I yield back the balance of my time.

THE CHAIRMAN:

Mr Dixon.

MR DIXON:

Thank you very much, Mr Chairman. Mr Hitz, I join those who are sorry to see you leave. I understand you are off to Princeton University. Regarding the Frogman case, you say that the CIA became involved mistakenly. As I recall, your report indicates that the attorney from CIA traveled to northern California and had a conversation with the prosecutor. I believe your testimony today reflects that you could find no written material by the attorney who, in fact, had that engagement with the prosecutor?

MR HITZ:

What we did find, of course, and I believe you are familiar with this, Mr Dixon, is the write-up that was made by the Office of General Counsel commenting on that particular exchange, that intervention with the assistant U.S. Attorney. The individual whom we think was involved in the actual negotiations, in fact, doesn't have a recollection of it.

MR DIXON:

And the write-up was not made by the person who was involved?

MR HITZ:

Well, we don't know that.

MR DIXON:

You don't know who it was made by? Is that right?

MR HITZ:

Correct. He has no recollection of it.

MR DIXON:

Now, you come to the conclusion that they interceded because of a mistake. And I believe the report indicates it is a mistaken identity of someone that the CIA did have a relationship with.

MR HITZ:

That's correct, Mr Dixon. We did not, the CIA did not get involved in the Frogman case until several years after the arrest took place. It came as a consequence of a cable, a State Department cable from Costa Rica saying that a private attorney and attorneys from the United States Attorney's office in San Francisco were about to come to Costa Rica to take the deposition of two signatories to a letter which had been directed to the U.S. Attorney's Office, seeking to reclaim the $36,000 that had been confiscated on Zavala's arrest. The letter came from what appeared to be Contra support groups, and one of the signatories, the agency mistakenly identified as an asset. It was a Hispanic name that was remarkably close to the name of an agent that had worked for us. In any event it was, as you suggest, a case of mistaken identity. Not having been able to locate the lawyer who was actually involved in this, and therefore not being able to speak to his or her mind set, it appears what they were trying to do was to protect the identity of the Contra support group's connection and in that way keep it from being revealed.

MR DIXON:

Did your investigation make an independent evaluation that this was a mistake or is this something that the CIA told you?

MR HITZ:

The CIA did not tell us, and in point of fact, we were the ones that discovered that the identity of the agent was mistaken.

MR DIXON:

Thank you Mr Hitz.

THE CHAIRMAN:

Ms Pelosi.

MS PELOSI:

Thank you, Mr Chairman. Again, I want to compliment you for having this open hearing, but I would request that we have another opportunity to question the Inspector General, because he will not be available long enough today for us to ask even a substantial part of our questions. In your judgment, was the contact between the CIA and the U.S. Attorney's office in this case, the Frogman case, appropriate?

MR HITZ:

There appears to have been a difference in interpretation of the propriety of the contact by the individual attorney who engaged in it. He stated in his write-up that he felt he was getting into an area that could cause embarrassment to the President's covert action activity in the Contra matter and drugs.

MS PELOSI:

My concern is whether the U.S. Attorney's office would perhaps not proceed in a matter for the reason you just said; to not jeopardize activities of the CIA.

MR HITZ:

Well, my experience with the U.S. Attorneys' offices has been, Ms Pelosi, that if the U.S. Attorney felt that he or she had a case in this matter, no intervention from the CIA would have warded them off. They would have gone for it and appropriately so.

MS PELOSI:

Mr Chairman, I know that we won't have much more time. So I'm not going to ask any more questions but I would like to make a couple of observations. As I listen to what you say, Mr Hitz, I appreciate you establishing your limitations: you don't have the power of subpoena, the guidelines weren't clear, certain things were not reportable at the time. For example whether an asset that we were engaged with was involved in drug trafficking. And that leads me to conclude that we may have unwittingly, and I use that word generously, we may have been subsidizing assets who engaged in drug trafficking. I'm glad that the law has changed, that now at least, it is reportable. But, I, for the life of me, cannot figure out why, as you say in your statement, that the CIA did not know whether these people were involved in drug trafficking. At least they should know, whether it is reportable or not, we at least should know. We are CIA. Shouldn't we know? Doesn't the pen say "knowledge is our business"?

MR HITZ:

We are pretty categorical on the issue of Blandon and Meneses and their lack of relationship with the CIA. Ricky Ross as well.

MS PELOSI:

I think that in our investigation we should talk to the people you couldn't subpoena. We could figure out why it wasn't worth $36,000 to go to Costa Rica for a deposition, and we can find out whether the CIA mistakenly identified somebody or not. This is not to say that within the limitations that you have in the Inspector General's office that you haven't made a good effort, but I'm afraid it keeps open some questions that I would hope that it would close.

But, nevertheless, thank you.

TEATRO PREGONES: The Twin Rigors of Art and Community, or Not the People Who Said Green

By Robert H. Leonard

SOMEWHERE IN THE HEART, Teatro Pregones is rooted in a concept of community that is way deeper than simple geography. For Pregones, community is a gathering of people around shared traditions, common culture and a commitment to theater as a place for ideas, growth and joining of forces. After all, Pregones started as a touring organization. Though the South Bronx has been the home for their creative work for 20 years, their first four years (1979-1982) were exclusively on the road, performing for Puerto Rican and Latino audiences throughout Connecticut, New York, New Jersey and Pennsylvania. They continued regular tours through this extensive region while building a series of creative partnerships in the Bronx until 1986, when they set up more permanent residence in St. Ann's Episcopal Church, in a South Bronx community called Morrisania. They have demonstrated their commitment to their home communities in the Bronx through several relocations since St. Ann's, yet they still tour today. They bring summer productions to nontraditional venues throughout the Tri-State area and schedule a variety of touring residencies across the nation that they arrange on their own and in collaborative partnerships with other ensembles. One of the most notable of these partnerships is called The Exchange, their ongoing, long-term creative collaboration with Roadside Theater from Whitesburg, Kentucky, and Junebug Productions from New Orleans.

Their strolling presence is consistent with the spirit of their name. *Pregones* is the Spanish word for the chanting of street vendors who walk from neighborhood to neighborhood selling their wares. Their roving consciousness also reflects certain distinct realities of the audiences they intentionally reach. Puerto Ricans and Latinos of all origins have come to the east coast of the United States, settling in various cities and towns, moving where opportunity suggests. The rich and complex artistic identity the company has developed, and Arnaldo López has so finely captured in his field notes, charts a fascinating interaction that can exist in a healthy artist/community relationship. What is particularly important is that this interaction, for Pregones, is neither defined nor confined by a specific geographic neighborhood or locale. In this reality, I believe that Teatro Pregones offers a challenging model of the artistic relationship with the world around it, a model that is useful in gaining constructive understanding of the crucial function of art: fulfilling essential human needs and the social impulse of community building.

Rosalba Rolón, the founding artistic director of the ensemble, is a pioneer. Her life work has taken the idea of contemporary American theater beyond the notion of simply producing seasons of plays. For Rolón, theater is the continuous exploration of a popular and accessible aesthetic, the development of style that comes out of a long-term artistic investigation of the culture and life realities of the audience, and the creation of "innovative and challenging theater rooted in Puerto Rican traditions and popular artistic expressions." The Pregones ensemble creates new theater works using any useful process and approach that particular projects may require. They adapt nontheatrical source material. They integrate dramatic text with music and dance. They utilize any number of other approaches that realize the specific artistic vision in actual performance and creative choices. Most important, Pregones ensemble members assume that their work is entirely and deeply integral to the culture of their audiences.

This reality expects and requires the constant education of the

Pregones production of Baile Cangrejero. From left: Soldanela Rivera, Waldo Chavez, Ricardo Pons, Jorge B. Merced, Alberto Toro and Desmar Guevara. Photo by H.L. Delgado

artists in the ensemble in order to deepen their understanding of that culture and how their own creative vision can be expressed in ways that are accessible and exciting for their audiences. This is quite different from the all too common assumption that new theater requires the education of the audience, that the audience has to learn how to appreciate plays, artistic choices, and innovative visions of performance.

Rolón's interview is particularly clear about artistic responsibility in relationship with community.

> ... audience and community are the same thing for us. Our audience comes from the community that we serve and, for us, community and neighborhood are not the same thing. Sometimes I don't know if people talk about community when they're trying to say neighborhood, or if they are talking about community in a broader sense. Plus, we may fall in the trap of thinking anything can be community: ten people think this is green, so it's the community who said "green." That's not it. The community is a very important, very specific social structure.

The continuous education of the Pregones ensemble includes the deep investigation of this social structure. A significant aspect of this structure is the multitude of institutions and agencies that constitute daily life in the community. Pregones' history is filled with creative partnerships with schools, churches, unions, groups of citizens organized for self-help projects, social agencies – a remarkable diversity of formal and informal organizations. Furthermore, the core ideals of Pregones as expressed in these interviews assume that ensemble members live their lives within the realities of the social structure – raising children, going to church, joining clubs and generally participating in the life outside of work.

In his interview, senior ensemble member and associate director Jorge Merced describes his entrance into the ensemble. Born and raised in Puerto Rico, Merced entered college as soon as he arrived in New York. In college he began to discover what he calls a "political restlessness" but "in the company of a largely Jewish North American community, a liberal left," not the Puerto Rican or even the Latino community. When he started working at Pregones, he was struck, at first, by the

> physical aspect to the work, meaning I ... had to walk, had to go to a specific place in the Bronx ... that put me in a different space, outside the safety-net of a college campus. And so, rather innocently, I begin to associate that with the community. Night after night I worked there with the company and started to see how many Puerto Ricans lived there, in the oldest neighborhood. Then I begin to identify, to appreciate what a community in the South Bronx was all about, and what it is that I do in there. In essence, my first few months with Pregones were very important because I was pushed to or forced to understand another space where dialogue among artists is taking place. I start to define community in those terms and before that I did not have that.

In some ways, then, Merced describes the social structure of the community in physical, even geographic terms. He goes well beyond that, however, when he also describes community as a "space where dialogue among artists is taking place." This is a constant theme in the interviews with the Pregones ensemble and a particularly important aspect of the Pregones model – a sense of a community of ideas, of the struggle for identity, of shared common interests that go beyond geographic terms. Merced shares insight through his subsequent embrace of this broader, deeper sense of community when he worked with children and young people in the neighborhood. Moving his own living quarters into the neighborhood near the theater, he realized,

> I take on the task of living and working in that community, with the understanding I then had about community, what it was, my misunderstanding of what it meant. ... Misunderstanding because it limited my perception of the breadth of the work one does; that [the work] is not determined or limited by the four, five or six blocks around the place where the show goes up. But it was crucial for me to go through the process of living there, teaching to kids and teens who come from Pregones' immediate surroundings. It was really important because we built close ties with the children, the parents ... . And, of course, the theater process gives way to the children's most intimate stories, so many of them heartbreaking. Because I identified in them a missing connection to identity, the definition of what makes you unique, what makes you yourself. They had no connection, the way I had no connection [to] growing up in Puerto Rico until I arrive at Pregones and I begin to understand how the world around me works. These children did not have that space, and when Pregones offers them that space for them to pursue their own questioning, it was a very intense period, both for them and for me. ... It was a beautiful project.

We can imagine the intensity of that beauty, as artist and child, teacher and student experience what it means to learn together, to share common discoveries, and to release them in the artistic expression of plays they create together. Allowing theater to be a "space" to give way to stories for common discoveries may be a simple way to describe the essence of Pregones' mission and practice. It also describes how the theater form can be a structure of the community, a mechanism for recognizing community, a way even for building community. Merced and his students grew together, despite their very different personal backgrounds, by discovering their common realities.

Wanda Arroyo, an audience member and clearly a fireball of energy, describes how her enthusiasm for what she discovered when she first encountered Pregones moved her to become an organizer of theater parties. She brings groups of friends and acquaintances (50 at a time) who come because they find it fun. They love to socialize, to dance and laugh together.

> That's one of the things that I love about Pregones, because everything is in Spanish and everything is cultural. ... I go and I enjoy it but I'm also learning. ... I'm surprised, I find myself thinking, "I never knew that" or "I never knew it could be like that." Plus I love the intimate connection between the actor and the audience. ... That made me feel at home, nothing to be afraid of.

This, to me, is a remarkable testimony to the accomplishment of Pregones, to have combined traditional cultural practice with innovation and discovery to stimulate learning and growth in a nonthreatening communal process. This is the highest of standards when it comes to assessing the worth and value of art in our lives.

The strength of Pregones' following has been proven to overcome, even ignore the impediment of distance. Pregones has moved several times since it first set up shop in St. Ann's. Each time, audiences have moved with it, confirming wide-spread satisfaction consistent with Arroyo's declared appreciation for Pregones' unique form of theater. Beyond the development of this kind of community support in the immediate neighborhoods of the South Bronx, a significant percentage of Pregones' regular audience travels in from further distances. "Forty-five percent come from Manhattan, Brooklyn, Queens and adjacent areas," says López.

Teatro Pregones

Location: The Bronx borough of New York City, N.Y.

Ensemble members: 4

Founded: 1979

Major activities: Creation of new work; Summer Stage; Main Stage; Visiting Artists; Teatro Matinee Cultural Connections; Conversations humanities forum; Asunción Playwrights Laboratory; La Ruta Panoramica presenting consortium; touring of repertory.

Facility: Owns its own 130-seat theater building on Walton Avenue just south of Yankee Stadium in the Bronx, with 2,400 sq. ft. work area for scenic and fine artists, four multi-use studios and administrative offices.

Annual budget: $1.5 million

Community Partnerships: Hostos Center for Arts and Culture/Hostos College and The Point CDC

Website: www.pregones.org

Company Statement

Teatro Pregones' mission is to create and perform contemporary theater rooted in Puerto Rican and Latino artistic expressions, and to present artists from diverse cultures, offering Latinos and other communities an artistic means to participate in society.

I asked audience members where they came from and confirmed that it is not uncommon for people to travel a distance to visit Teatro Pregones. Upstate and out-of-state families make the trip regularly. … It is not so much where they live but where they meet, and why they meet, that matters.

López goes on to identify why Pregones has become "a signal landmark," a place to meet for so many from so many places.

People spoke of Pregones as an organization they can trust. Programming was repeatedly described as "genuine," "honest" and "true." … "I trust Pregones because they speak my language," offered one patron, "because I know they like to eat their *tostones con mojito*. That's why I think people will come in here with their guards down – it's safe. But it's not just about that. It's not like at the bodega or at the [Puerto Rican Day] parade. You're not gonna leave the same way you came in.

How does the ensemble earn this trust and how does it accomplish artistic events that affect, even change their audience's perceptions, understanding and sense of the world with such surety and consistency? By diligent, professional, smart application of hard work. The discipline of Pregones, says López, "obeys the twin rigors of artistic vocations and commitment to community." The interviews of Pregones ensemble members and associates burn with this rigor and the joy it brings them. This is an ensemble of highly skilled, professional artists who are on fire with their commitment to community.

An especially revealing reality in this ensemble is that it is made up of Puerto Rican artists who were born, raised and trained in Puerto Rico, then moved to the U.S. and, in near equal measure, Puerto Rican artists born, raised and trained in the U.S., for whom English, not Spanish, is their first language. The differences between the native Puerto Ricans and the Nuyoricans constitute the realm of "the other" just as rigidly as any other cultural collision. The interview with José Joaquín García exposes the hard, challenging work the performer and the ensemble undertake with each new ensemble member. The substance of the problem García faced is not only language in all its manifestations but gesture, common understanding of the world around us, and common practice in relating to all the people in it. García's joy in mastering Pregones' required skills and vision is mixed with a remembered pain at the cultural gulf he experienced as he struggled to find his way into the ensemble. Besides the quite beautiful story that he and the other ensemble members recount in these interviews, García's journey marks a strong pathway for thoughtful, effective cultural education. Recognizing, honoring and crossing cultural boundaries is a life skill that is increasingly required of all who live in the United States (and the world, for that matter). Certainly theaters and arts organizations are faced with these challenges as a matter of simple survival, if not as a central function of their purpose. In this, as in its artistic accomplishments, Teatro Pregones is a model of exceptional value, offering challenge, courage, and pathways for many, regardless of specific cultural background or orientation.

The process of bringing new members into the ensemble, a process of acculturation, parallels the creative process of adapting traditional texts into contemporary performance – a signature process for Pregones. Jorge Merced describes a moment when he realized the substance of this process.

> Understanding that all [the popular sources and materials] are a part of us and that we can own them, use them, take advantage of them, see them upside down, inside out, that is something I hadn't done until then. I didn't understand that, in fact, within the codes of so-called folklore or the so-called cultural identity of a community or of an ethnic group, or even a country, one may find the tools to craft a new voice without sacrificing that which is dear.

It is fascinating to understand these two stories in parallel, to hear how the processes of gaining performance mastery within a new culture resonate with the processes of making new art from existing texts and other sources and materials. Each process confronts that which is often considered somehow "untouchable" – uh oh, can't go there. Pregones removes the taboo and accepts the difficulty. Besides vision and courage, this work insists on discipline or, as many Pregones' members call it, rigor.

The interview with senior ensemble member and Associate Director Alvan Colón Lespier defines with clarity the depth of training and the constancy of continuing education that the Pregones ensemble requires of itself to do its work. Beyond, or perhaps, around the classroom, workshop and rehearsal space, the ensemble's artistic "inheritance" includes Puerto Rican poets, visual artists, as well as theater practitioners, political activists, artists of all disciplines and community leaders from throughout the Caribbean, Mexico and Central and South America. This is a company that actively draws on global sources to create theater with their audiences gathered locally. Colón's passion and intensity when describing what theater is for him, as a consequence of this amalgamation of the world onto the stage, resonates truthfully in the imagination. Acknowledging, in his own words, the dual intentions of the ensemble – the artistic, aesthetic with the political, ideological – Colón proposes the image of discovery as an orientation for his sense of theater: "Discovery in the sense of removing the veils that cover the issues of our time...." Given Colón's deep appreciation for this image, it is gratifying to the reader (as it must be to Colón himself) to hear so many audience and performers echo the image in their own stories about the ensemble. Recounting conversations with many people surrounding Pregones, López says, "Coming to Pregones for the first time was often described as 'an awakening,' 'a discovery,' or 'a revelation.'"

Pregones proposes the human experience of discovery of self and the world. The art of Pregones is inseparable from its community. This does not mean its neighborhood. It does not strictly mean its lingual home. Rather it means the community from which its audience springs, the people who share with Pregones common trust, hope and joy.

An excerpt from "El apagón" (The Blackout)

Basada en el cuento / based on the short story
"La noche que volvimos a ser gente"
Por / by José Luis González

Adaptación / adapted by Rosalba Rolón con Jorge Merced &
Alvan Colón Lespier

Dirigida por / directed by Rosalba Rolón

Protagonizada por / featuring Jorge B. Merced & José Joaquín
García

Dirección Musical / musical director Desmar Guevara

Músicos / musicians Desmar Guevara, Waldo Chávez, Pete
Emilio Rodríguez

Escenografía / set design by Regina García

Luces / lights by Alvan Colón Lespier

Updated script, completed and revised by Jorge B. Merced on
9/20/2002 © Pregones Theater

(El pianista y el bajista entran al área de los músicos y comienzan a tocar la introducción de Noche de Ronda. Luego se iluminan los actores en la barra y el trompetista en el área donde comienza a tocar la melodía. La canción se acompaña de varios apagones que capturan a los actores en distintas posiciones en el escenario. Terminada la música los actores comienzan el texto. Músicos acompañan el texto.)

Actores:

¿Que si me acuerdo? Se acuerda el Barrio entero si quieres que te diga la verdad, porque eso no se le va a olvidar ni a Trompoloco, que ya no es capaz de decir ni donde enterraron a su mamá hace quince días. Lo que pasa es que yo te lo puedo contar mejor que nadie por esa casualidad que tú todavía no sabes.

JORGE:

Pero antes

JOSÉ:

... let's have a beer

JORGE:

... bien frías

JOSÉ:

... cause its so hot

JORGE:

... quién quita que hasta me falle la memoria.

JOSÉ:

Ahora sí, salud y pesetas. Y fuerza donde tú sabes. Well it's been a few years and I could even tell you the months and the days, porque para acordarme no tengo más que mirarle la cara al barrigón ese que tú viste ahí en la casa cuando fuiste a procurarme esta mañana. Yeah, yeah, the older one, who is named after me, but if he had been a girl we would have had to call her Estrella o Luz María o algo así. O hasta Milagros, mira, porque aquello fue ...

JORGE:

Pero si sigo así voy a contarte el cuento al revés, o sea, desde el final y no por el principio, así que mejor sigo por donde iba. Bueno, pues la fecha no te la digo porque ya tú la sabes y lo que te interesa otra cosa. Resulta que ese día le había dicho yo al foreman, que era un judío buena persona y ya sabía su poquito de español, que me diera un overtime porque me iban a hacer falta los chavos para el parto de mi mujer, que ya estaba en el último mes y no paraba de sacar cuentas.

JORGE & JOSÉ:

Que si lo del canastillo, que si lo de la comadrona ... ahhh!

JORGE:

Ah, porque ella estaba empeñada en dar a luz en la casa y no en la clínica donde los doctores y las norsas no hablan español y a demás sale más caro.

JOSÉ:

At four o'clock I finished my first shift, y bajé al come y vete ese del italiano que está ahí enfrente de la factoría, cuestión de echarme algo a la barriga ...

JORGE & JOSÉ:

... hasta que llegara a casa y la mujer me recalentara la comida, ¿ves?

JOSÉ:

So I had a couple of hot dogs and a beer, while I read the Spanish newspaper I had bought earlier in the morning, y en eso, cuando estaba leyendo lo de un latino que había hecho tasajo a su corteja porque se la estaba pegando con un chino, at that moment, mira, I don't know if you believe in these things, pero como que me entró un presentimiento. (MUSICA) I felt that something big was going to happen that night, I just didn't know what. Yo digo uno tiene que creer, because go figure, what did the Latino, el chino y la corteja have to do with what I felt. Porque no fue que lo pensara, que eso es distinto. Bueno, pues acabé de mirar el periódico y volví rápido a la factoría para empezar el overtime.

JORGE:

Entonces el otro foreman, porque el primero ya se había ido, me dice:

JOSÉ:

Are you planning to become a millionaire and open up a casino in Puerto Rico?

JORGE:

Así, relajando, tú sabes. Y vengo yo y le digo, también vacilando: No, si el casino ya lo tengo. Ahora lo que quiero poner es una fábrica. Y me dice:

JOSÉ:

What kind of factory?

JORGE:

Una fábrica de humo. Y entonces me pregunta:

JOSÉ:

And what are you going to do with the smoke?

JORGE:

Y yo bien serio, con una cara de palo que había que ver: ¡Adiós! ¿Y qué voy a hacer? ¡Enlatarlo! Un vacilón, tú sabes, porque ese foreman era todavía más buena persona que el otro. Pero porque le conviene, desde luego. Así nos pone de buen humor y nos saca el jugo en el trabajo. El se cree que yo no lo sé, pero cualquier día se lo digo para que vea que uno no es tan ignorante como parece. Porque esta gente aquí a veces se imagina que uno viene de la última sínsora y confunde el papel de lija con el papel de inodoro, sobre todo cuando uno es trigueñito y con la morusa tirando a caracolillo.

JORGE & JOSÉ:

Pero, bueno, eso es noticia vieja y lo que tengo que contarte es otra cosa.

JOSÉ:

Pues como te iba diciendo, después que el foreman me quiso vac-
ilar y yo le dejé con las ganas, pegamos a trabajar en serio.
Porque eso sí, aquí la guachafita y el trabajo no son compadres.
Time is money, ya tu sabes. (Movimiento y música.) Pues,
pegaron a llegarme radios por el assembly line y yo a meterles los
tubos. Yeah, that's what I used to do; put the tubes in each radio;
two in each radio, one on each hand. Al principio cuando no
estaba impuesto, a veces se me pasaba un radio y entonces,
muchacho, I would have to run after it y al mismo tiempo
echarle el ojo al que venía seguido, I thought I was going to go
crazy. Cuando salía del trabajo sentía como que llevaba un baile
de San Vito en todo el cuerpo.

JORGE:

A mí me está que por eso en este país hay tanto borracho y tanto
vicioso. Sí, chico, porque cuando tú quedas así lo que te pide el
cuerpo es ron o algo así, y ahí se va acostumbrando uno.
(Música/vals) Yo digo que por eso las mujeres se defienden mejor
en el trabajo de factoría, porque ellas se entretienen con el chis-
morreo y la habladuría y el comentario, ves? y no se imponen a
la bebida.

JOSÉ:

Bueno, pues ya yo tenía un rato metiendo tubos y pensando
boberías cuando en eso viene el foreman y me dice: Hey, someone is looking for you. Yo le digo: Who, me? Y el me dice: Of
course, there is no one else here by the same name. Entonces
pusieron a otro en mi lugar para no parar el trabajo y ahí voy yo
a ver quien era el que me buscaba. Y era Trompoloco (MUSICA)
... que no me dice ni que hubo sino que me espeta:

JORGE:

¡Oye, que te vayas para tu casa que tu mujer se está pariendo!

JOSÉ:

Sí hombre, así de sopetón. Y es que el pobre Trompoloco se cayó del coy allá en Puerto Rico cuando era chiquito y según decía su mamá, que en paz descanse, cayó de cabeza y parece que del golpe se le ablandaron los sesos. There was a time when I met him in the Barrio that he would just start spinning until he'd get dizzy and fall to the ground. De ahí le vino el apodo. (MUSICA – Harmónica) Eso sí, nadie abusa de él porque su mamá era muy buena persona, médium espiritista ella, tú sabes, y ayudaba a mucha gente y no cobraba. Uno le dejaba lo que podía, ¿ves? y si no podía no le dejaba nada. Entonces hay mucha gente que se ocupa de que Trompoloco no pase necesidades. Porque él siempre fue huérfano de padre y no tuvo hermanos, así que como quien dice está solo en el mundo.

(MUSICA – Canción de Trompoloco)

MÚSICO:

¡Oye, que te vayas para tu casa que tu mujer se está pariendo!

JORGE:

Ay mi madre, ¿y ahora que hago? El foreman, que estaba pendiente de lo que pasaba porque esa gente nunca le pierde el ojo a uno en el trabajo, viene y me pregunta: What is the trouble? Y yo le digo: No, nada, que viene a buscarme porque mi mujer se está pariendo. Y entonces viene el foreman y me dice: Really, then what are you waiting for? Go home? Porque déjame decirte que ese foreman también era judío y tú sabes que para los judíos la familia siempre es lo primero. En eso no son como los demás americanos, que entre padres e hijos y hermanos, se insultan, y hasta se dan por cualquier cosa. Yo no sé si será por la clase de vida que la gente lleva en este país.

(MUSICA)

JOSÉ:

Siempre corriendo detrás del dólar, como los perros esos del canódromo que ponen a correr detrás de un conejo de trapo. ¿Tú

los has visto? Acaban echando el bofe y nunca alcanzan al conejo. Eso sí, les dan comida y los cuidan para que vuelvan a correr
al otro día, que es lo mismo que hacen con la gente, si miras bien
la cosa. Así que en este país todos venimos a ser como perros de
carrera.

JORGE:

Bueno, pues cuando el foreman me dijo que qué yo estaba
esperando le digo: Nada, ponerme el coat y agarrar el subway
antes de que mi hijo vaya a llegar y no me encuentre en casa.
Contento que estaba yo ya, sabes, porque iba a ser mi primer
hijo y tú sabes como es eso. Y me dice el foreman: Hey don't forget to punch your card so that you can get paid for that half hour
you have been working for, cause from now on you are really
going to need the money. Y le digo: Como no, y agarro el coat y
poncho la tarjeta y ... Trompoloco, estaba allí mirando las
máquinas como eslembao: ¡Avanza Trompo, que vamos a llegar
tarde! Y bajamos las escaleras corriendo para no esperar el
ascensor y llegamos a la acera, que estaba bien crowded porque
a esa hora todavía había gente saliendo del trabajo.

JOSÉ:

¡Maldita sea, y que tocarme la hora del rush! Y Trompoloco que
no quería correr.

JORGE:

Espérate, chico, espérate, que yo quiero comprar un dulce.

JOSÉ:

Bueno es que Trompoloco es así, ¿ves? como un nene. He's good
at running errands, simple errands, or washing the steps of a
building or anything else that doesn't require much thought. Pero
si es cuestión de usar la calculadora, entonces búscate a otro. Así
que vengo y le digo: No, Trompo, que dulce ni que carajo. Eso
lo compras allá en el Barrio cuando lleguemos.

JORGE:

No, no, en el Barrio no hay de los que a mi me gustan, Esos nada mas se consiguen aquí en Brooklyn.

JOSÉ:

Ay, tú estas loco ... y en seguida me arrepiento cause that is the only thing you can't call Trompoloco. Y se para ahí en la cera, más serio que un chavo queso y me dice:

JORGE:

No, no, loco no.

JOSÉ:

No, hombre, si yo no dije loco, yo lo que dije fue bobo. Lo que pasa es que tu oíste mal. Avanza que el dulce te lo llevo yo mañana.

JORGE:

¿Tú estas seguro que tú no me dijiste loco?

JOSÉ:

Seguro, hombre.

JORGE:

¿Y mañana me llevas dos dulces?

JOSÉ:

Mira, bobo y tó lo que tú quieras, pero bien que sabe aprovecharse. Claro, chico, te llevo hasta tres dulces si quieres. Y entonces vuelve a poner buena cara.

JORGE:

Está bien, vámonos, pero tres dulces, acuérdate.

JOSÉ:

Y yo, caminando para la entrada del subway con Trompoloco

detrás: (A Trompo) Sí, hombre, tres. Después me dices cuáles son.

(MUSICA – Actors freeze momentarily and then exit the stage. Musicians continue. At the end of music, José re-enters.)

JOSÉ:

So we ran down the stairs and went in the station con aquel mar de gente que tú sabes cómo es eso. Yo iba pendiente de que Trompoloco no se fuera a quedar atrás porque con el pushing y shoving a lo mejor le entraba miedo y ¿quién iba a responder por él? ¡Muchacho! ¡El Expreso! (Grabs Trompo by the hand and brings him center stage.) Prepárate y echa pa'lante tú también, que si no, nos quedamos afuera.

JORGE:

No te ocupes.

JOSÉ:

Y cuando se abre la puerta y salen los que iban a bajar, nos metemos de frente y quedamos prensados entre aquel montón de gente que no podíamos ni mover los brazos, which was a good thing cause we didn't have to hold on to the poles.

JORGE:

Oye panita yo como que estoy un poquito azorao, con todo este gentío ...

JOSÉ:

Y así seguimos hasta la 42, and then we transferred because we had to get to 110th Street and Lexington. Y ahí volvimos a quedar como sardinas en lata.

(MUSICA)

JORGE:

Entonces yo iba contando los minutos, pensando si ya mi hijo habría nacido y cómo estaría mi mujer.

JOSÉ & MÚSICOS:

(SINGING)

Su amor es como un grito

que llevo aquí en mi alma

y aquí en mi corazón

(JORGE JOINS)

y soy aunque no quiera

esclavo de sus ojos

juguete de su amor ...

JORGE:

Y de repente se me ocurre: Bueno, y yo tan seguro de que va a ser macho y a lo mejor me sale una chancleta. Tú sabes que uno siempre quiere que el primero sea hombre. Y a la verdad que eso es un egoísmo de nosotros, porque a la mamá le conviene que la mayor sea mujer, para que después le ayude con el trabajo de la casa y la crianza de los hermanitos.

(ALL SING)

Usted me desespera

Me mata me enloquece

Y hasta la vida diera

por vencer el miedo

de besarla a usted.

JOSÉ:

Bueno, pues en eso iba yo pensando, and feeling very much like a father when all of a sudden ... ¡fuácata!

(APAGÓN – BLACKOUT. Music explodes and then slowly dies down.)

JOSÉ:

¡Ahí fue! Que se va la luz y el tren empieza a perder impulso, slowly losing power until it stops right in the tunnel, between stations. Bueno, de momento no se asustó nadie. You know that the lights go out in the subway all the time and it is no big deal. En seguida vuelven a prenderse y la gente ni pestañea.

JORGE:

Y eso de que el tren se pare un ratito antes de llegar a una estación tampoco es raro. Así que de momento no se asustó nadie.

ROADSIDE THEATER: Little Epiphanies

By Ann Kilkelly

IN MICHAEL FIELDS' INTERVIEWS and profile of the company for "Performing Communities," Roadside Theater's veteran company members speak passionately and politically about their own long-term connections to work and the organization they have built. There is a powerful sense of mission in the interviews, and deep, often disturbing reflections on the theater, the place and the work in an ever more challenging national context. Roadside has carefully documented its considerable history. The collection of interviews and reflections here offers what Roadside's Donna Porterfield terms "little epiphanies" – the surprising and significant emergence of individual voices within the particular imperatives of this context and geography.

Just getting to Roadside Theater and Appalshop in Whitesburg, Kentucky, is a mythic journey through miles of curves, coalfields, kudzu, green slopes and hollers. Erica Yerkey and I made a site visit to Roadside during Appalshop's Seedtime on the Cumberland Festival in June of 2002. We wanted to supplement Michael Fields' interviews and profiles by visiting this important festival in a geographical location close to our own in western Virginia. I subsequently made a separate visit to a few of Roadside's community partners, whose remote locations made it difficult to schedule during Fields' visit.

Stepping out of the car, we walked immediately into the middle of a parade in downtown Whitesburg, a phantasmagoria of huge puppets made of trash bags, fire engines and townspeople on motorcycles. In the next several hours, we sat on hay bales to hear a live radio broadcast of mountain music, visited the "Kids Bored Café," heard four different gospel groups from the region, viewed the premiere of an Appalshop documentary about musician Ralph Stanley, saw Roadside's production of Ron Short's "South of the Mountains," and New York artist Marty Pottenger's "City Water Tunnel #3." Only a few of the events were specifically produced by Roadside, most were by Appalshop; the theater sits in the heart of the larger organization's building and complex organizational structure. The mission to preserve and develop the heritage of the region launched the theater and the organization, and this mission is still the focus of a deliberately constructed community.

Literally and otherwise, Roadside wrote the book about working in and for community; and the group profile shows dozens of performances and projects over more than 25 years. Dudley Cocke co-authored "From the Ground Up" and Roadside created "A Matrix of Community Arts Practice," both foundational texts in the field. As they themselves articulate it, Roadside is about place and new work generated in it – stories and songs of the central Appalachian Mountains and their economic realities. Roadside has also used highly "local" knowledge and practices to create and put to good use models that work very far from their literal home; they have accordingly had an extensive influence on the field.

Mining for Ghosts

Story forms the basis of Roadside's methodology, their processes well articulated in company materials. Roadside's assessment of its own methods and the successful link to political change and community well-being locates the story itself as key. The story passes through visible and invisible communities in the telling – we hear the voice and the personality of the individual, so hearing and listening is a profoundly located experience. Yet, in its ability to conjure or cite the community (of the moment or of the past), the story cedes the authority of one expert individual (playwright) to empowered multiple voices. The accumulation of "little epiphanies" in songs and stories becomes the performance

Roadside Theater, Pregones Theater, and Junebug Productions performing in Promise of a Love Song. Photo credit: Jose García

of the community.The point of arrival through story is also, therefore, a democratic political gesture, the telling a gesture of civic responsibility.The great Irish author James Joyce said that the short story is an "epiphany." He used the notion of journey and arrival from the Catholic Church's Holy Day, which celebrates the arrival of the three wise men at Christ's birthplace. Joyce saw that moment metaphorically as the arrival of a character at a new point of consciousness or awakening. The moment is also a defining point of identity, like the narrator's in Joyce's "Araby," or the protagonist's in Roadside playwright Ron Short's "Pretty Polly," one of Roadside's signature pieces

The stories told in a group interview with Roadside's core members (Dudley Cocke, Donna Porterfield, Tamara Coffey and Ron Short) feel like surrogates for others that have been told many times and still others that may not be told in this context. Michael Fields gestures towards these ghostings in his remarks about what happens when the tape recorder is turned off.

... Road stories including: Alabama prison show pranks,

Swedes and alcohol, Danes and beer; Vietnam; the fact that everyone should have to do some national service; why some folks can work in an ensemble and others can't; musical practice – physical practice; grants and why we don't get them (threatening), more respect and why we don't get that (too strange and need more money); school systems; the necessity of collective action; back to road stories – Swedes and telegrams; more road stories – a beautiful Brazilian woman in red and salsa music; the need for more reflective time in our work.

The passage suggests not only layers of past epiphanies, but also an acute sense of pleasure in the telling, a quality present in many of Fields' interviews with company members. The shared conversations reflect and often focus on Roadside's purposeful evolution from a small group of similarly committed individuals to a highly organized arts institution. The passage above also suggests Fields' relish, clearly also felt in Roadside company members throughout the interviews, of digging through the detritus of shared and individual cultural experiences to get at who they are, then and now. A common thread through the reflections on the past and the present moment of the interviews is a palpable and grounded sense of the value of the conversation itself, especially the conversation as it opens the space for the trading of stories, anecdotes and analytical thinking.

Roadside members practice what they preach, and they tell stories in response to questions. For example, when asked how she came to work in community arts, Donna Porterfield tells the wonderful story of her father, who, as a child, made plays for the farm animals.

When I was a little girl I lived on a farm in West Virginia. My father was raised on the same farm. He always loved any live performance. From the time he was a little boy, he would make shows with the farm animals, and make his cousins be in them and stuff like that. When he got older he wrote plays and did them with the church youth group. They weren't religious plays but they let him do it. My mother and brother didn't like that so much, so my father would always take me to any live performance there was anywhere. I had seen a good deal of theater when you add it up over time. Then we moved to northern Virginia, off the farm, and saw theater people usually think of: Arena Stage, Catholic University. When I was out of college, I came here to visit a roommate of mine from college. Her husband worked at Roadside Theater. We went to a Roadside Theater performance – this was about 1975 – of "Red Fox/Second Hangin'." That was the first full-length play that Roadside did. It just bowled me over because I realized that of all the theater I had seen, for the first time I was seeing theater that was from my background, from my class background, from a rural sensibility – all these things that I had never seen. I think the theater that we do here, and the theater that we work with other people to do in their communities, is that. It's their own stories from their own background, and how you make theater out of that. That's the kind of grassroots theater that I think of, and that's what's important to me. That's the reason. A little epiphany.

Tamara Coffey follows with an animated description of her family's impromptu and frequent music sessions; she says they kept many instruments around for people who dropped in, even a bass in the hall closet! Both Coffey and Porterfield connect their growing awareness of "theater" as something outside their home communities and experiences until they encountered Roadside. Coffey says:

> I had dreams of going off to New York and working with "the real theater." And when I was in college working in college theater, it was fun, but I didn't see it going anyplace. I didn't see anything happening out of it, and went through a lot of different things in my life, and got an opportunity to go and see Roadside.
>
> The first time I met Donna and Dudley and Ron, I actually came in for a show they were doing up at the elementary school at Pound and it was "Pretty Polly." It just blew me away. After I talked with Donna and Dudley the next day I

realized that I had seen, "Red Fox/Second Hangin'" on the public television station in Kentucky probably three or four times and had just loved it. And never connected it with somebody from here, for some reason. It really was such a sharp thing. It was just so real, and I could see what was going on there. I just begged and pleaded until they let me come and work here.

Cocke argues that the connectedness Coffey feels and articulates is the essence of their theater.

With Roadside, I'll just say that the theater came to be because form, content, audience and place were linked at the inception of the theater. So, that linkage of form and content, audience and place at the very beginning has allowed us to be an experimental theater because it has given us a firm foundation upon which to make new work. That is what we do. All our work is original work. Each piece is different than the piece before it. All the pieces have a root, a strong root in this heritage, this place.

Ron Short describes the growth of his own understanding of grassroots theater and its relationship to other kinds of theater and to outside economic pressures in the following passages.

Personally, I think one of the more interesting things for me, after being in this work for awhile, was going around and seeing other theater, that I never would have seen had I not been able to use this work to propel me in my travels throughout the country. One of the curious things that people ask me is, "There is no tradition of theater in the mountains that you come from. Where in the world could art come from in a place that has a long history of poverty and a long public kind of popular belief that people are backwards?" I just am amazed by that, obviously, because there is so much drama in everyday life here. Our lives are just filled with drama, by constant drama. In church, the thing that most people understand the least is the potential to see theater in some ways at its best – theater of long history, of storytelling. In my church they tell stories, so I'm amazed

Roadside Theater

Location: Whitesburg, Kentucky (pop. 1,600)

Ensemble members: 7

Founded: 1975

Major activities: Creation of new work; touring plays and workshops; performing community cultural residencies; mentoring new theaters; creating video and audio productions; publishing books; helping create community developed plays.

Facility: Part of Appalshop, which owns two buildings in Whitesburg that include office space, warehouse, 150-seat theater, gallery, and film and video editing suites.

Annual budget: $400,000

Community Partnerships: Social and civic clubs, public schools, social-service agencies, arts presenters, historical societies, the medical community, folk artists, churches, colleges, and individuals.

Website: www.appalshop.org/rst

Company Statement

Roadside Theater is a professional ensemble theater located in the heart of the Appalachian Mountain coalfields of rural eastern Kentucky. Since 1975, the company has been writing, performing in its home theater, and touring nationally (and occasionally internationally) original plays drawn from the history and rich culture of its mountain home. Roadside Theater is creating a body of drama based on the history and lives of Appalachian people and collaborating with others nationally who are dramatizing their local life. It is the character of Roadside's relationship with its audiences that defines its work. Roadside's audiences are a broad cross-section of the American public, including a significant number of habitual theatergoers as well as many attending professional theater for the first time.

that other people sometimes can't see the theater here in the ways that we see it. Naturally it amazes me that they will look elsewhere before they will look in their own place. All the speakers from this group interview talk about the difference between their approach and a mainstream idea of theater, one they learned about and saw in school or in commercial media. By definition, that theater was distant, outside local geography or experience. Then came the realization that the story embedded in the life of ordinary people was theater and had a legitimate place in what we call culture.

It is important to underscore that part of Appalshop and Roadside's work for many years has been to undo the class and regional biases in so much mainstream culture. This recognition seems less dramatic now than it did 20 years ago, with cultural criticism only beginning to take apart the systemic structures of prejudice, yet the necessity and analysis remains extremely pertinent. Roadside presented a very early and very radical challenge to longstanding concepts of poverty and class in the region. Moreover, their programs and productions countered the canned versions of Appalachian life that too often stand in as representations of regional cultural. In these important passages, Short makes us understand that such biases are deeply embedded in theatrical forms as well as in straightforward social behavior and institutions. Roadside's work has been central in working to expose the depth and nature of such prejudices and to create a public place for the beautiful real voices of the region.

> When you live outside of those boundaries you don't have any of that political control, that economic control, even the control of your own image. Somebody else is controlling and telling you who you are. Then the only thing that you have is your own story. That's about the only thing that you have. It comes down to how do you use that in a public way. That's essential to me. Theater is the last public forum for common people. We still can have access to it. You don't have to have the huge corporation. You don't have to have the technology of television. It is a place where common people, everyday people, can get up and speak their mind and have other people listen to them. That process of dialogue with the audience enters into the collective consciousness of that community and helps shape that community. As it uses the collective knowledge, it gets built together.
>
> For me, that's what grassroots theater is. It's about having a voice. A public voice. One which demonstrates not only, "This is what I think and feel," but, "I'll speak it in the public forum and then I'll wait for a response so that we can have a dialogue about that." We can continue then to formulate our thoughts and change and grow as we need to in

our own community. But it will be driven internally. It will come from within.

Fields writes that interview conversations often make reference to the men's experience in and of the war in Vietnam. Ron Short makes the connection of his own brutal experiences with his ongoing desire to make theater. Short talks about casualty reports during the Vietnam war, the numbers offered in the news to "assess" wins and losses. He, someone "in country" witnessing these reports, decries them as having little or nothing to do with the experience of the individual human. He says that if you are the one hauling away bodies or "up to your knees in a rice paddy," the abstractions of numbers, of wins and losses, cannot represent your experience, but in fact, offer a horrific counter-point. And he says that in such urgent life situations, you interrogate reality and yourself at the deepest level. "What the hell am I doing here?" His sense of the theater as "the last public forum" connects an implicit idea of outrage and resistance to the need for story. Short implies that the voices of those who do not make war but are required to fight or who do not control economic policy but must bear the consequences of it, can be re-bodied or re-imaged on a stage or in a performance environment.

The act of imagination, bodied forth in story, therefore becomes a collective political action, originating, as Short said earlier, "from within." This telling of the individual life experience in a public, artfully and musically arranged, representation, differentiates what Short sees as his own theater work and what he criticizes as "popular culture." He uses the term to excoriate predigested commercial television and other mass produced forms, which have no legitimacy because they manufacture, in order to sell, a homogenized "mythos" that keeps the real stories suppressed. He says: "And then I think there is a whole hidden world of America that people never see. And I do believe that community theater, or grassroots theater is that other voice. It's that voice that never gets a chance to speak for itself or demonstrate itself in a real way."

In a way that Short himself calls "mysterious," despite the

careful articulation of methodology by all members of the company, the public stories that Roadside find, create, and catalyze the unheard and unseen of past and present toward public presence and being.

What's Reponsibility?

Donna Porterfield tells a succinct version of Roadside's evolution into residency as the basis of their work with community and connects with the importance of story in their process. In early days, Roadside made a large percent of their income touring, and they asked themselves how to serve the audiences that emerged who reported never having been to the theater. She says:

> And so we were saying well, we've got these people there. This isn't working. What's responsibility? And how do they get integrated into these arts programs? That's when we all talked about it, and Ron really pushed it that we need to do community residencies. We need to stay in the community longer. We didn't exactly know what that meant right then. We had some ideas. We decided that we would go for that. Our booking partner was from Southern Arts Associates and we all thought this was economic suicide, you can never do this, it's too expensive. Our booking partner said, "Yeah. Let's do it. It's important." She believed in it. That was Theresa Holden. So we did. And at that time we were able to raise money and start doing these things.
>
> We started doing one of these residencies, and booking was a lag time, in Dickenson County Virginia where Ron grew up and where we have a really strong audience for our work. Right over here, the next county over from where we are sitting. We were doing a residency with a high-school drama class and a teacher. They were crossing over and working with a senior center and all these different things were coming about. We started talking about how can you get people talking to each other and telling stories again. It used to happen all the time, as Tamara mentioned, in these different places, and it doesn't anymore, naturally. So, how

can we come up with a way of that happening? We came up with a story circle, developed a story circle, which all the methodologies and written material have to go on. Anyway through this residency we started to figure out how we could make arts participants rather than arts spectators out of the audience. ...

We got better at it. And as we got better at it we started writing it down because it started making clear sense to all of us. And we wrote it down, everyone in the company. At one time we had nine people on full-time salary, and everyone produced residencies. It didn't matter what job you did, you were a residency producer. The methodology that we had, that we all agreed on, that was the way we were going to do it and the place we were going to go. ... We all did it in a little bit different way, but we got to the same place.

Porterfield's passage reveals how thoroughly Roadside has come to understand the significance of residencies in communities. It is also clear that their own working methods function as grassroots development for themselves. When Cocke, therefore, makes the following brief definition of the theater, the process that got Roadside there is visible.

Those are two important characteristics of our theater, accessibility and commitment to place. By commitment to place we mean commitment to the people here, the culture here, the heritage here. And that commitment leads to the responsibility to make that heritage new, to reinvent it. That's what the fun of theater is.

Community partners make extensive commentaries in the interviews about their valued relationships with Roadside. Most see Roadside as having led them to their own discoveries. They have come to see story as a core concern, of story, songwriting, music and public performance as important tools. Roadside partnered with the Mountain Laurel Center in a project about dealing with cancer and health issues. Director Marilyn Maxwell provides an analysis of the importance of art making for their organization. She describes its 'place' in the organization's values.

I think that storytelling and theater is of critical importance to our vision and dream for this Mountain Laurel Cancer Research and Support Center. In fact, in our planning and what we've done, I mean, we've got our information and education component, and we've gotten that funded. We've got cancer help system. We've got the University of Virginia's College at Wise that got a grant funded with some staff there. Then we need a planner for the center. But what we think is the soul of the whole thing, and if we've lost it we have lost our soul, is the theater and storytelling component. We think that is what grounds us in the community. That is what makes us human. That is what makes us reach out and try and be inclusive. It is that tool of the theater.

Maxwell's "soul" is similar to Cocke's notion of the "fun" or pleasure of the theater in the re-invention of culture. In a piece like "South of the Mountains," it is pretty clear that pleasure, enjoyment is there for the audience in the way that theater provides an anchor, a connection to the emotional and compassionate, to the undefined but crucial "soul." Other groups call this "glue," but it is the work of the imagination here that is sufficiently complicated and accessible to be inclusive and mysterious.

It is a mark of success that these projects, such as this one and the one about domestic violence with Hope House, are credited to Roadside and individual members, but feel completely "owned" by the community organizations. There is no sense of individual ownership, either psychologically or economically, by the artists, although their leadership and skill is not only cited but understood. This marks what I see as the fulfillment of the deepest mission of community arts work, the ability of the community group to integrate and own arts practice for themselves. In my interviews with various partners, I heard directly about health issues or sexual abuse as it came through stories, retold in this new context. The work Roadside helped perform allowed individuals and groups to talk more freely about issues long after the initial performances. This remarkable effect is a result of the time spent in articulating and practicing the practice. Art in story catalyzes more of the same – stories generate more stories. Then, stories become important means to generate discussion. Discussion and more stories create a cycle of dialog and exchange.

Often community partners can cite long-term change and lasting vivid memories of the impact a particular piece or project has had on them. David Raines, a teacher who was engaged in a four-year school residency project with Roadside, comments extensively on the activities and the educational value of the projects. Student Crystal Raines (no relation, but serendipitously working as a waitress in the state park where we met) recalls a songwriting workshop and story circle she was involved with several years previously. They both describe a session wherein a group of boys discovers that they can make a song from the history of a coal-mining disaster in their town. She says, "I remember how it starts: 'Way down yonder in Convict Hollow miners worked to earn a dollar. Then one day in '23 there was a bad catastrophe.' I can remember that!"

The familiarity of the ballad shape creates an ease and playfulness reflective of the process, when it finally started to work for the boys, who had been struggling to write anything at all, who were having trouble in school in general. As in so many mountain ballads, the incremental repetition and the singable quality of their song framed the retelling of an event that probably still has economic consequences that may not be consciously perceived. David Raines asserts the value of the residency in this way:

> Students from poor backgrounds that often don't have a lot available to them, have parents with very little education, and very often are not successful in school, for obvious reasons. Storytelling and theater-type work is geared to helping students from that background more than anything. I mean they normally struggle in writing things down. They don't write well, they don't have good vocabularies, they don't express themselves well. ...
>
> We saw students that normally struggled greatly in writing and reading do well with lots of these type endeavors. I felt like it was a great thing because of that.

The creation and sharing of songs is also a core practice, completely woven into Roadside's story telling practice. The rich history of the region's music gives the work character and emotionality that are mythic. The songs make direct linkages with the songs and dances of other cultures, such as the Zuni people in one of Roadside's partnerships. The ballads and the voices create a beauty that communicates history and experience beyond written language. This beauty coexists with very intentional politics. For instance, at Seedtime, Roadside produced Marty Pottenger's "City Water Tunnel #3," Ron Short and Kim Neal's performance, several gospel groups, some white, some black, some racially mixed, within the same 24-hour period. The sense was dizzying; sometimes the theater felt like a very traditional Christian church environment, sometimes like a performance art house, sometimes like a classroom, and sometimes like a community-center performance space or a church basement. None of this is accidental, and the profusion of events, each in itself only somewhat detached from its usual "locale," has a power to create a kind of community in which many kinds of voices can be present. Such successes are therefore always complicated, and, by design, free or affordable, marrying multiple perspectives to accessibility.

Even with the kind of success Roadside can legitimately claim come challenges, and these too are palpable in the interviews. Often gripping and funny by turns, Roadside's personal stories sometimes seem diminished within the complex structure the organization has grown into. The passion for serving the region and creating community has not visibly dimmed, and the organization continues to generate more partnerships and projects. Yet there is a sense of impatience and exhaustion with impact of the current recession on the national arts scene.

I see a gap between the work generated by communities and the original performance work generated by the company. People remember signature pieces "Pretty Polly" and "Red Fox Second Hangin'," but such large ensemble pieces now seem less possible as discrete productions. Although present company members have been there for a long time, the number of performing artists in the company seems to have narrowed substantially. Is this a loss or a fulfillment of mission? Is a new generation of artists coming into the work? Has enough of the art-making process been transmitted or will this take care of itself as community members take on more and more projects? Such questions are not so much critiques of produced work, but concerns that face many of the ensembles in *Performing Communities,* especially those, like Roadside and Carpetbag, that formed at a point in U.S. culture where political activism and critique could engender healthy debate and federal and state resources. WagonBurner's Debbie Hicks and Roadside performers bring up the "canary in a coal mine" figure to express their sense of that the endangerment of the arts foreshadows more profound losses; indeed we have come to see them since these interviews.

Roadside has found structures that allow symbiotic relationships to prosper in their regions, despite the often cited cuts in national arts budgets and the increasing "anti-art" sentiments so many of the interviewees discuss. Cocke tersely remarks he "can't imagine not having the struggle." Yet the "little epiphanies" set in motion in shared stories and experiences continue in audiences and because of community projects. Although Roadside has been incredibly successful in garnering foundation and grant money, their economic future and the particular structures they have built (like all middle sized arts organizations) is deeply threatened by changes in funding contexts and public organizations. Yet Roadside is a model for models – the dissemination of their methods and values seems to me assured beyond the present, in the seeding of many projects that are now growing their autonomous methods of using art and story.

An excerpt from "South of the Mountain"

By Roadside Theater

Written by Ron Short
Original music by Ron Short
Directed by Dudley Cocke
Cast: Tommy Bledsoe, Ron Short, Nancy Jeffrey Smith
© Roadside Theater 1982

A Note About the Play

"South of the Mountain" is set in the central Appalachian Mountain coalfields of Dickenson County, Virginia during the period of 1945 to 1955. The characters are: Thad, a Dickenson County native, who is 20 to 30 years old; Thad's wife, Mabel, an eastern Kentucky native who is five years younger than her husband; and Eb, Thad's older brother, a bachelor who never left the family farm. The age of the characters varies with the particular story they are telling. All three are on the stage at all times. Costumes are simple, reflecting the dress of the day. The scenic and lighting designs vary according to venue: from the simple for a community center to the complex for a large auditorium. Properties include a roughly hewn wooden bench, two plain wooden straight-backed chairs, and a small table. Musical instruments – fiddle, banjo, and guitar – when not in use are placed within the set. Roadside Theater premiered "South of the Mountain" in 1982 at Appalshop in Whitesburg, Kentucky. From 1982 to 1997, the play toured nationally and internationally with the same ensemble cast.

THAD:

I shunned the coal mines as long as I could. I always kinda dreaded gettin' started in 'em. I just didn't like the idea of goin' underground. I guess I'd been walkin' 'round on top of it too long. But, that's all the work there was around, 'ceptin' farming and I knowed where that would get you.

MABEL (enthusiastically):

In the coal camp they was houses on each side of the holler, and the houses was connected.

THAD:

One great big row of houses on one side

MABEL:

and one great big row of houses on the other.

EB (disparagingly):

There was no separation between the buildings, just walls. You see, it saved the coal company money by not having to have a wall and a roof for each house. Just one big long house.

THAD (disregarding Eb's sarcasm):

One side was called the Titanic

MABEL:

and one was called Noah's Ark.

THAD:

Right down at the end of all them houses was a big company store.

MABEL:

There wasn't no hospital, but they was a doctor's office.

THAD:

All furnished by the coal company,

EB:

but they got ever' cent of it back. 'Cause they wouldn't let you get ahead.

THAD:

The coal company furnished your housing, electricity, had the commissary for the food . . . but they took it outta your pay.

EB (disgusted):

And they paid you so little hit wadn't much more than a labor camp.

MABEL (laughing):

You talk about a raggedy, black bunch of younguns from fightin' through the coal camp from one end to the other in the coal dust in the summertime, and all the mud in the wintertime. From hand to mouth, they just lived.

THAD:

It got to where we had to go to the store each day and buy what we could draw in scrip for that day's work.

MABEL:

Then you'd go back the next day. I'd buy a pound of soup beans and cook 'em

THAD:

and go the next day

MABEL:

'cause the man had to work the next day for to get some more scrip.

EB:

I've heared people say they'd rather do anything than hoe corn

THAD & MABEL:

so that's what we done!

EB:

It was hard to tell when they was workin' and when they wad-n't.

MABEL (exuberantly):

But people follered it and lived with it right on up.

THAD:

Up to that time, in the mountains, people had never been that close to where people was a-makin' some money.

EB (exasperated):

Money, money, money. That's all you ever talk about. They wad-n't but one man that I remember ever'body kinda talked about as havin' any money, and that was old man Henry Whitt. He had got shell shocked in the Army, during World War One, I reckon, and he drawed a pension. Seemed to me like it was about thirty dollars a month, and that was total disability.

But Henry kept a bull. (Thad steps up protectively to Mabel; this is rough talk.) Wadn't many people had enough money where they could afford to buy a bull, and when you took your cow down there to Henry – I mean to his bull – that'd cost you a dol-lar, that is if she got with calf, otherwise it didn't cost you noth-in'. But, they wadn't many people that had that kinda steady income.

MABEL (angrily speaking up for herself):

There's a difference between wantin' and needin'. When you want the things you can't have, then you're poor!

EB:

Yeah and they's a difference between wantin' and gettin'!

(Thad and Mabel separate. Thad moves to far stage right, Mabel to far stage left.)

MABEL (to audience):

We started kinda fixin' the house up, him with a regular income. Got linoleum for the floors, curtains, a new couch, things like that. He was makin' good money, but it was hard work.

THAD:

They was somethin' funny 'bout the whole thing right there from the start, best I could figure. They needed all this coal to generate all this power, but I have shot many a cut of coal with a breast auger – that was a drill where there was no power whatsoever. You cranked her by hand. You'd drill, shoot, and load your own coal for a dollar a car, nothin' for the rock, and you handled as much rock as coal. You didn't use nothin' but a pick and shovel. It was the sweat, muscle, and blood of the coal miner what generated the power for this country.

EB:

When Thad first started workin' in them mines told me he figgered he'd just get a little money ahead and get out. But he never did seem to get money ahead.

THAD:

For the first time in my life, I got credit. It wadn't much, just a little ole store up from the house. Feller kept a "runnin' tab" on you. I went in once a week and tried to catch up to it.

MABEL (apologetically):

It was easier that way so you could send the kids. We just got the things we needed, meal, flour, sugar, lard, stuff for his bucket.

THAD:

Yeah and they's real glad to write it down on your tab for you. Besides that, you never had no money in your pockets.

MABEL (turning to audience):

'Til we got the refrigerator you couldn't keep nothin' fresh. We'd keep milk and butter in the root cellar, but in summer it wouldn't keep long. You had to can or pickle ever'thing you raised. You couldn't keep leftovers – you eat 'em or they was fed to the animals. We'd never had ice. After we got the refrigerator, we'd just make ice water 'cause it tasted so good. I made ice cream for the kids. Used to, you could buy this mix from the store and make ice cream in the ice trays. That refrigerator sure made things a lot easier.

THAD:

We used carbide lights then. It was a pretty rough go.

EB:

Hits a wonder they hadn't been a lot more men killed than there was. Said sometimes the roof was so low you couldn't even take a drink settin' up.

THAD:

Lots a times you had to lay down on your side so you could tilt your head back. But that smoke from the dynamite was worse. That stuff'd make you so sick.

EB:

There wadn't enough air in the mines to push it out.

THAD:

Give you a headache to where lots of times you'd have to come out just for the like of air. No dust control. Coal miners eat the dust, that was your dust control. You couldn't see your hand before you or nothin' else with all that dust.

EB:

I don't know why it didn't kill a man in thirty days.

MABEL (appealing to audience):

With an electric stove you can cook a meal in half the time it takes on a woodstove. When we got ours, there was a special deal where you got an electric mixer too. I always liked to bake, and this made it so much easier you wouldn't believe it. They come out with cake mixes that most cases was better than cakes baked from scratch. Canned biscuits, too. We didn't like 'em too much, but I bought 'em ever' now and then.

EB:

First car in our family, I reckon he bought it.

THAD:

It was a Chrysler, which just about put us in the poor house, deeper than we was. I give $75 for it. That was the most money I'd ever had.

EB (laughing):

Hit was worth maybe 75 cents.

THAD:

Yeah, I'd a-been better off without that Chrysler.

MABEL (suddenly remorseful, near tears):

I've seen him come in with his clothes froze stiff on his body where he'd worked in them water holes, got wet, then come outside. Then, when he could get a ride, ride home in the back of a truck in the middle of winter. I've seen him come in, where I could have cried he looked so pitiful. But even still, it was better than not havin' a job at all. You had to make it one way or another. (Suddenly going to Thad) But I always vowed if ever there was any way that I could get him out of them mines, that I was goin' to do it.

THAD (rejecting Mabel's coddling):

Hush now. Shore it was dangerous, ever'body knowed that. I've seen it fall, and I've had it to fall around me. I was loadin' one day, and looked up and seen the shimmer on the top. I started to run, and a big slab come down and the coal car caught it. That was all that kept it from catchin' me. You constantly lived with that. It was just a way of life. You didn't question it. They wadn't no other work around. Tried not to think that much about it.

You didn't run out askin' for help. A job was all you asked for. I got ulcers though, and never could get rid of 'em long as I was in the mines. Kept a vomitin' and vomitin', couldn't eat nothin'. Atter John L. and the union come in, we got medical benefits, so I went over to see this doctor in Harlan. He took some X-rays and run a bunch a tests on me, and he told me, "Go hunt you a job outta them mines. You get out of 'em and stay out of 'em, if you want to live."

(Song – sung and played on guitar by Thad)

Running on Empty
I'm leaving these mountains
So far behind.
My money's all gone.
There's no work to find.
I'm all out of patience,
And about out of time.
And my heart
Is running on empty.

I never thought
That I'd see the day
I'd leave my wife
And my kids this way.
My woman she don't
Have a word to say,
'Cause her heart
Is running on empty.

(Chorus)

Hey mister a job is all I need.
I'll work for you 'til my fingers bleed.
I can stand the pain, and I can live with the greed,
But I can't keep running on empty.

I cuss the day
That I left the mines,

And I cuss the day
That I went down the first time,
'Cause that ol' coal dust
Will make you blind
'Til your heart is running on empty.

(Chorus)

(Repeat 1st verse)

WAGONBURNER THEATER TROOP:
Laughing at the Edge
By Ann Kilkelly

THE SPEAKERS IN THESE MATERIALS about and by WagonBurner Theater Troop are satirists, historians, writers and storytellers. They have no single location, no building and no set organizational structure. They are very aware, with W. E. B. DuBois' "double consciousness," of Native American identities within the white man's world. They can perceive and make visible in their theater the "edge" where the difference of given and chosen native historical communities meets the dominant system. They make work with brass-tacks humor, visionary and shared leadership, and a very deep sense of what theater is and does for Indian communities. Robert Leonard did interviews in at least four locations, from Washington, D.C., to Rosebud Reservation in South Dakota. In these interviews, company artists fashion an astute and particular portrait of this company in much the same fashion that they create performance work: They talk around and through issues and ideas, they echo and reinforce each other, they use complex cultural analyses, stories and humor. Like the implicit and edgy joke in their name, they play off and with culturally defined stereotypes and ignorance about Indians and Indian culture.

Liz Hopkins, a playwright from the Rosebud project, says, "What I try to show people is that this is what happened to us." Their methods involve 'talking story,' collective writing, editing and performing; they collect gags and antics that reveal and mock the absurdity and horror of history; and they provide a writing/letting that helps individuals cope with difficult situations and connect to memories and cultural histories that are sustaining. And what flashes off virtually every page is the pleasure, the fun of the process. They say that Indians need laughter, and they set out, intellectually and habitually, to create it.

One Size Does Not Fit All

The results of WagonBurner's relatively short life span and the nature of their work do not register well in a "one size fits all" kind of survey, according to Director LeAnne Howe's frustrated reaction to the "Performing Community" survey. There is a small body of work, a limited audience – if you start counting, not much adds up. There is a subtraction process that takes place in the very act of accounting and quantifying, a process reflective of white culture.

This sense of speaking and writing in tension with a culture and language that doesn't fit comes up frequently, as interviewees critique the process they are engaged in, even the interview itself. Debbie Hicks offers an eloquent analysis of the problematic term "effective" in response to interviewer Leonard's question about a Project Hoop workshop with LeAnne Howe.

> Are you saying "effective ways" in terms of if we had a deadline and we need to efficiently use our human resources to meet that deadline? Say we are putting a proposal forward for a reviewer or a funder – no, that would not be effective. But if you are saying "effective" in terms of retaining that authentic voice – yes.

The question of effect or impact often assumes impacting a broad, mainstream, "white" audience whose values, tastes and needs can be predicted. There is not necessarily a single audience of any kind, however, assumed in WagonBurner's work, and Hicks uses the term "authentic voice" to characterize the specific "Indianness" of the project, its variation, its difference. Her sense of what that means is specific and complicated.

> Understand too, there we were this handful of southern and eastern Native persons in a small Native community that was primarily western peoples or northern peoples, who

Wagonburner Theatre Troop performance of "Indian Radio Days" at the National Museum of the American Indian in New York City, NY, 1995. Left to right: Brenda Lynch, Claire Cardwell, Justin Data, Debbie Hicks, LeAnne Howe, far right. Photo credit: member of Wagonburner Theatre Troop

again didn't always interact harmoniously. Within the little Indian community there within Iowa City we were trying to create our own niche. We were trying to create for ourselves a sense of belonging or continuity. Those were ironies that would play back into the stage. LeAnne and Scotty had their own sense of what it meant to be Choctaw in a Choctaw language community. We had other cast members who had a strong sense of what it meant to be Indian, but it was rooted in that intertribal pow-wow community that develops in urban communities but has now spread as an archetype of Indian-ness, especially in the south and the east where you have so many deculturated rural communities.

Tribalography

Leonard writes in his field notes that this company has found a way to be independent and function outside many theater structures. Indeed their feistiness flies off the page. I see them, additionally, as using the very oppositional structures they work against to foreground cultural identity. Director Leanne Howe says:

> This is what I like to think of as "Tribalography." American Indian playwrights, actors, storytellers create stories form the experiences of our people, and ourselves. In that sense, our work belongs to the ancestors, ourselves and the next seven generations. WagonBurner Theater was, and continues to be a community of Indian artists and Indian activists who enjoy working together, mentoring younger Indians, and, who merge art and activism as a teaching tool for Indians and non-Indians.

The discussions of the specific playwrighting process always connects identity to the specifics of story telling and the remarkable group editing that a number of participants cite. Here is Hicks' description:

> Over hours of meandering discussions, returning back to the thread. Sometimes heated discussions. Offering, drafting characters and plots on a yellow note pad as we were speaking and then playing them back, acting them out, discarding, offering suggestions and moving on and agreeing to come back and meet again another time. Maybe having a really exciting meeting and then coming back the next day, sleep-weary and bleary and coming back with revisions to offer.

WagonBurner's playwrighting processes are utterly stunning in simplicity and success. There is a telling interview passage in which Howe describes how she gets folks to come and write. She has been talking about the difficulty some teachers have in recruiting students:

> So, the way I work is with the collective. We just get everybody. Go out in the yard and get people and say that we are going to write a show. This was with one class. Get that old man sitting out front and come in. So, we start talking, and

we write collectively together line for line. Just start talking. And then they'll say, "Oh we are writing a play. What does she say now?" So, he typed, I typed so that we would have two different records into our laptops. They wrote the play. It got real big and we had to bring it back down, which they figured out for themselves.

Liz Hopkins, a playwright, comments on the integration of the act of "playwrighting" and community life:

LeAnne talks about that all the time. Indian people will sit there and talk a subject to death. That is what happens in the play. They talk, they discuss it, they throw out a theory. They might eat in between. They'll have this meeting of the minds. Then, when everyone has had their say, they will come to a conclusion and everyone seems to accept that. That is how it is. No one says, "Okay, that is it." But in our hearts, that is it. There is nothing more to say. That is how that play came about. That is true. Native Americans, we do sit there, we talk, we eat, we laugh. Maybe somebody might get mad. Maybe somebody might cry. There is a lot of therapy in Native American talking circles, [as] they used to call them. I think there is a lot of therapy in that. People work out their frustrations, or express their thoughts.

Howe, the company's director, offers the metaphor of the "amoeba" to relate the fluidity and sustainability of the creative process:

So, in some ways, what we offer as an alternative model is sustainable – you know, things don't have to be in stone for them to be together. I think of it like an amoeba. It comes together, it expands, it grows, it explodes. We expect it to be very difficult. Our expectations are already very bad, so we will manage somehow. We will come back together and it will be very fluid, elastic.

WagonBurner artists consistently see their creative work deeply entwined in the fabric of their daily lives, whether its immediate manifestation is a production or not. The way performance is defined here structurally resembles the perform-ance-studies distinction Richard Schechner makes between traditional stage drama, based on one solo authored text, and "social drama," much broader in its contexts and relevance. Interestingly, the performances of "Indian Radio Days" and others incorporate this idea in their creation, but are not ethnographic in the forms they take.

The fluidity and elasticity allows a pastiche of improvised and set materials to take form within a basic set-up like the Bingo Game, a known and practiced form in Indian communities. These known forms, often imposed by the mainstream culture and adopted by Native Americans, lend themselves to satire and parody. The most provocative and powerful theme in the interviews, is, I believe, this understanding and constant presence of humor, laughter and critique in the collaboratively created performance work.

The Best Medicine

WagonBurner participants speak frequently and at length about the value and impact the various theater projects have had in their lives. The word "therapy" comes up – most talk about the freedom and pleasure of self-expression. And the stories connect to ancestry and history, helping with reclamation and the laborious reconstruction most Native people face after centuries of deculturation, relocation and disenfranchisement

Satire traditionally employs exaggeration and irony in a framework offering serious social criticism. Parody is a related form that copies the form of a genre or style to reveal its absurdity. Both occur in WagonBurner's stories, where laughter may expose social ills or provide a survival mechanism. Performer Dee Antoine comments:

> Laughter is the best medicine. I think that is how a lot of people deal with it. For some of them it is hard for them to talk about it, but if they do, it is in a joking manner. It is not too personal. I think the feeling right now is that people

WagonBurner Theater Troop

Location: Dispersed across U.S.

Ensemble members: 20

Founded: 1993

Major activities: Creation of new work; workshops; touring repertory.

Facility: Borrowed or donated space in various places.

Annual budget: $3,500 to $14,500

Community Partnerships: Sinte Gleska University Art Institute, Rosebud Reservation, South Dakota; CSPS Theater Cedar Rapids, Iowa

Website: none

Company Statement

Wagonburner Theater Troop's mission is to continue to exist as an American Indian theater group. In the 21st Century we will continue to create and perform American Indian plays.

want to get them out there and deal with them. The Uncle Wannabuck and the Uncle Prayalot is referring to medicine men, some of whom are dipping into other people's pocket to pay for sun dances. That is wrong in our tradition. People are bothered by that. The Mormons coming and taking the children away, they are bothered by that and they want some way to express it

Antoine's term "medicine" invokes healing, and others use stories to face hard truths and challenges. Nancy Whitehorse tells a story about going to the "Megadrop" to challenge herself, and the dialog between Antoine and her is itself an example of the process of generating story and commentary with embedded irony and edgy humor:

NW I went to Minnesota at the beginning of the month. I always like to challenge myself because everything is always a challenge. For example, my marriage, it is totally nonexistent. I knew it was going to bottom out. It was going to be something scary, something brand new for me. So, I rode this ride called the Megadrop.

DA: I rode that before.

NW: About 12 stories. You sit on these chairs, your feet are dangling and it goes up. I would watch and it would hang there for 15 seconds and just drop.

DA: Quickly.

NW: For me it was a challenge to myself. If I can get on that at 40 years old, when my life feels like it is unraveling, get on there and drop. Well, it went up. It went up faster than I thought, and when it got up there I thought, "Oh shit I've got five seconds."

DA: Can't change your mind.

RL: Can you bail out?

NW: No. You are up in the sky. And I didn't want it to drop. I thought, no, no, no. And then I heard that click. I counted to five and that was it. whooooooooooshhhhhh.

DA: That is life, too.

NW: Yeah. That is how I looked at it. When I come home that is how the bottom of my life is going to drop out, to say, well I survived that drop. It was sickening. It was fast, it was sickening, I had no control over it. And then to come back here with that experience and everything does drop out. Hmm. How come I am not crying? How come I am handling it a lot better than I thought I would?

DA: Gaining confidence.

NW: When my feet touched the ground after riding that ride I felt like a peppermint patty, you know? It was like a pull all the way down inside. Whoa. So, I went and tried a couple of more rides. I'm scared of heights. That is how I was able to take care of a lot of stuff without someone telling me, you need to go to codependency. "You are an abused woman, you need to go to codependency to try and understand why this person is doing what he is doing and why you are feeling what you are feeling." Not everybody needs that. People, for me, this person just needed to write something down. Take all these thoughts and put them down on paper. Not touch it, not revise it. Get up walk away from it, do it again and then go back maybe in a few days and read and say, "Oh God, you are pitiful." Writing this kind of theater for me was damn good therapy. I think I am funny. I can't help that. I've got this mother and father the same way, and all these brothers and sisters. To have someone like LeAnne say, "That is great! I never heard that before!" It was great. It made you feel like you did matter. You know? If you know what the life on the rez is like, even though you struggle real hard to keep the bad things out of your life, this is the rez. It swamps you like a big wave. It just takes you and you have to crawl out again.

Whitehorse not only adroitly analyzes how this kind of courageous and dangerous self-challenge constitutes a therapy (to her) more valuable than the lame talking therapies of the omnipresent AA meetings, but she casts the whole into a perfectly shaped and mythic story. The mythic is decidedly not the romantic, but is about contending with "the rez." In the comedy is also the tragic; in fact, it would be hard to find a better definition of tragedy that Whitehorse's remark, "It swamps you like a big wave. It just takes you and you have to crawl out again." This relationship of the funny as it relates to and is the tragic, is described by Howe:

It is just like, the world could be falling apart and something could happen. We might not laugh about it then, but we will later when we tell it. It might be something inappropriate. It might be something that was really sad, but Indian people need to laugh. We need to have something to tie us down when we are really low. And we are ready, we are always ready for a laugh. That is a really important part of our society and our culture. Anywhere you go, Indians want to laugh.

Satire, of course, evokes social critique through laughter and the outrageous, and the efficacy of satire is discussed in several interviews. Satire depends on using offensive stereotypes as offensive; it therefor requires that the audience members recognize the technique. In a couple of cases, audiences, often non-Indian, have mistaken the constructed image (an absurd "symbolic" icon concocted of gummy bears and chicken feathers) as real Indian spirituality, suggesting how powerful the racialization of the Indian has been, to use Toni Morrison's term. Groups of white women, most of whom were fairly politicized over gender issues and who were well educated, were offended that "Indian Radio Days" didn't offer a "legitimate" workshop in Indian spirituality. Of course, the company performed the workshop satirically, playing the trickster role and calling into question the very assumptions of a workshop designed to "teach" Indianness in a few hours. Implicit in the story is also the realization that "Indian spirituality" was precisely what the white man set out to destroy.

This particular experience, told by performer Debbie Hicks, reveals challenges of performing for white and Indian audiences. There are many different tribes represented in the company, though most of them are from Southeastern tribes. They recognize and analyze the many differences of the Indian people in their audiences, and they also try to face pressing problems internal to the Indian communities, such as sexuality and poverty. The use of satire doesn't work predictably. Some native groups take offense at the stereotypes, asserting that the performances reinforce negative images in an offensive way, portraying Native people as buffoons or giving insult to some notions of sexual identity.

They do court the edge, deliberately. As hilarious as the image of the Bingo Lady handing out Salvation Army clothes as "prizes" actually is, it is a painful reiteration of experience for reservation audiences. White audiences may recognize the insult in their own "charity." Indians may laugh in recognition of a behavior that has demeaned them. The hilarity of satire, in time-honored fashion, exposes, in an ostensibly "palatable" way (thinking of Jonathan Swift) the viciousness of human behavior. Laughter, in this case, at Princess Wannabuck or the Bingo Lady, involves an acknowledgement of what the satire reveals. Such edgy comedy has a feeling of payback and analysis. The act of acknowledgement, of saying, or feeling "Yes, I understand," while splitting a gut laughing, seems like an incredible balancing act, or, a trickster's magic that has power to sustain curiosity and satisfy anger.

Liz Hopkins reflects:

> What I try to show people is that this is what happened to us. And now you are going to see it from a different perspective. We tried to have ceremonies like Lakota people and that is exactly what the Father would do. He would come in and set up a table and serve a Mass during our ceremonies. They do things like this, totally inappropriate, and have no respect for what they are trying to do. Yet, I wanted to show it so that everything is turned around. See that is what I am trying to show people. It is not anger, but I want them to have a different thought: "This is what we did."

What Happens Next?

Those interviewed do not see staying together as a challenge – they want more theater, they are split apart in time and space, taking care of their lives, earning livings – but they believe that WagonBurner will come together in its own time when there is a project that must be done. And the interviews themselves are evidence that the stories continue to evolve and change.

At one point, Director Leanne Howe says, "And you just have to think. If I did that, how come I'm not running this country now?" Although she is referring to the absurd mythologizing of Indian power, I am convinced that she could, and probably should, be running things. For the ability to see time in relation to growth and cooperation, just as in the playwrighting process, is, in itself, a requisite for change.

An excerpt from "WagonBurner Theater Troop: An Evolving Indian Theater Experience"

By WagonBurner Theater Troop

Introduction by LeAnne Howe

With contributions by Jodi Byrd, Claire Cardwell, Justin Data, and Ken McCullough of the WagonBurner Theater Troop

LeAnne Howe (as herself), July 2002:

Out of the experience of Indian artists and activists coming together to work on Indian Radio Days, WagonBurner Theater Troop (WTT) was born in 1993. Indian Radio Days was a play that the late Roxy Gordon and I wrote in the summer of 1988. WTT began to perform the play, but its members also begin writing new scenes for the play, improvising and in a way, creating a new Indian Radio Days with each and every performance. This is what I like to think of as "Tribalography." American Indian playwrights, actors, storytellers create stories form the experiences of our people, and ourselves. In that sense, our work belongs to the ancestors, ourselves, and the next seven generations. WTT was, and continues to be a community of Indian artists and Indian activists who enjoy working together, mentoring younger Indians, and, who merge art and activism as a teaching tool for Indians and non-Indians. Performance and dramatic acts abound in American Indian tribal cultures. In the Southeast, storytellers were performers. But so were Lakota warriors. Lakota scholar Craig Howe has shown how Counting Coup is dramatic reenactment, a performance of wills many tribes on the Great Plains participated in. Anthropologist Harvey Markowitz

has pointed out that Winter Counts, things told, is a Lakota performance involving pictures and words. English professor Dean
Rader has said in his forthcoming book "Speak to the Words,"
co-authored with Janice Gould, that Native poets in the
Southwest conflate poetry, prayer, song and ritual into one powerful poetic moment that enacts language. In other words performance.

Another example I can think of comes from the Choctaw *anolis* who would perform a story for an audience, and eventually
call on their audiences to interact or become part of the performance. As Cyrus Byington, Missionary to the Choctaws, from
1820- 1865, wrote:

"There was a well-known, solemn style appropriate to all
speeches delivered in public (by captains, councilors and chiefs.
It abounded in serious words, called by some, 'speech-terms.'
One part of a sentence was nicely balanced by another. It was
poetic in style and manner of delivery. At the close, that orator
would invite the people to listen to him, and to consider what he
had said. '*Nanta hocha*,' 'What is it?' Or '*Nana Hona*,'
'Something,' [the audience would respond]. Pausing a moment,
the audience would give loud responses of, '*Yummah*' 'That is it';
'*Alhpesah*,' 'It is right.' They would repeat this four times, and
thus preparation was made for the announcement of the main
subject. While speaking they [the orators] rarely looked anyone
in the face.

What I think Cyrus Byington is trying to describe is a kind of
interactive theater performance in which the Choctaw *anoli* or
teller cues the audience to recollect certain events, and the mood
the event evokes. This is called foreshadowing in playwriting.
Foreshadowing is a classic storytelling device that creates sus-
pense by alerting the audience to expect that a certain kind of
story is coming. The events that followed worked on the performer and audience to create a kind of cultural glue that binds
a culture. Today in Choctaw Country (Durant, Oklahoma) I've
worked with high-school Native playwrights and performers,
who interactively engage their audiences in much the same way
traditional anolis did. They worked together to write their

plays, then collectively directed their performance, then engaged their audiences during the performance.

Wagonburner Theater Troop called on all these same traditional life ways to perform. We came together to tell stories, engage an audience, and interact with them and each other. I believe Wagonburner Theater Troop's experiences inform the "American Indian never-ending-story." This may seem a tall order, but given the remarkable circumstances that American Indians have found themselves in over the last 510 years, nothing is impossible. Look for us. We're coming to your theaters soon!

Some Remarks from Wagonburner Theater Troop Members:

Ken McCullough (himself), July 2002:

For me, personally, there's no point in trying to identify a favorite part of IRD ["Indian Radio Days"], since there are so many excellent moments – from the commercials, to the "Bingo Lady," to Joseph Flaming Attire, to Kevin Kostner in "Son of Dances with Wolves," to the serious historical vignettes. To a large extent, the success of these bits is tied, in my memory, to what the actors brought to them. For example; Steve Thunder McGuire does a perfect parody of the real Costner.

So I'm going to address my specific remarks to a segment on which I collaborated; namely, the interview of Claudine Levi-Ecofemme by a nameless host, who is meant to be a parody of William F. Buckley. On his show "Firing Line" (here it's "Firing Blanks" – referring to the impotence of the interviewer's remarks as well as to the U.S. Cavalry), Buckley, the ultimate conservative WASP, made a habit of trying to snow his guests, particularly if they represented a minority, by using elaborate Latinate phrases, and name-dropping. I worked with South Carolina Educational Television, which produced "Firing Line," so I had first-hand opportunity to see Buckley in action. He also had the characteristic of being almost reptilian when he sensed a weakness in a guest – you could see him eyeing his or her jugular. Having spent four years at an eastern prep school as a "scholarship student," I'd developed a serious aversion toward elitism of the Buckley ilk.

Jodi Byrd (my collaborator) and I thought it would be amusing to pit this Buckley clone against an Indian ecofeminist, who would counter his line of B.S. with a line of ecofeminist jargon. I had been on the fringe of the academic world for some years, and Jodi was in the midst of it, being a graduate student at the University of Iowa, and both of us had acquired a healthy disdain for academic jargon and Bucklian babble. Both characters spin out of control and are revealed to be charlatans, to some extent, though the interviewer to a greater degree. It was fun developing this bit because the dynamic in the repartee was slightly different from the rest of IRD, though it still used the interviewer-interviewee format. And it temporarily shifted IRD into an egghead mode. These two characters more closely resemble the parodies in Vizenor's "The Last Lecture on the Edge," though Vizenor himself has come under fire as being a self-parody, in that he talks the talk but doesn't walk the walk. Like other academics, he knows the material but isn't engaged in the life. We can see that Claudine Levi-Ecofemme might be headed in that direction.

Claire Cardwell (herself), July 2002:

My fav scenes!

FEMALE ANNOUNCER:

(Hit bell)

You're listening to AIR's production of Indian Radio Days. The time is now 29 minutes past the hour. Coming up next hour is The invasion of the English, French and the Germans.

Audio Direction:

FADE OUT "INDIAN OCEAN"

NARRATOR:

I'm now standing on a rock. I dare say it could be the Plymouth rock from all appearances. Who are you, sir?

INDIAN CHIEF WHO MET THE MAYFLOWER:

(Cup your hands together like you are hollering at a boat way in the distance.)

No! No! NO!!!!!! We've got to send you back! It would only encourage others like yourself to attempt this dangerous and foolhardy trip across the ocean in these flimsy boats. Besides we don't have the room. And who knows what will happen next? You may try and take our jobs, and drive the price of corn to an all – time low. No, No No. You must go back!"

NARRATOR:

Who are you People?

INDIAN CHIEF WHO MET THE MAYFLOWER:

I'm one of the Indians who met The Mayflower.

AUDIENCE DIRECTION:

Boo & Hiss

NARRATOR:

So it's untrue that you welcomed these poor English prisoners and debtors with open arms to the New World for an American Thanksgiving Dinner?

INDIAN CHIEF WHO MET THE MAYFLOWER:

What do your think, fellow?

NARRATOR:

Well, this is not what we're taught in the history books, so I did-n't know.

INDIAN CHIEF WHO MET THE MAYFLOWER:

Fellow do you mean history books or dime novels?

(Turn to the Audience and holler again.)

No. No. Go back. That's right. I'm afraid you cannot stay. I'm sure Captains Pete Wilson, Rush Limbaugh and Newt Gingrich will understand.

NARRATOR:

I am in the final battle of the Mousse-Argonne French Campaign, 1918, during World War I. I am talking with Simone Anolitubby; another Choctaw from Oklahoma. She is a soldier in the United States Army. How did you get here, soldier?

ANOLITUBBY:

I enlisted, SIR.

NARRATOR:

What's an Indian doing here?

ANOLITUBBY:

I am a good American. I fly the American flag. I am a code talker, SIR.

NARRATOR:

A code talker? What is a code talker?

ANOLITUBBY:

One day, a Captain John Smith, our commander happened to over hear us conversing in our language. He said, "Corporal, how many of you Choctaw do we have in this battalion?" I said, "We have eight who can speak Choctaw fluently, SIR." So he said, "Round'em up on the double. We're gonna get these Krauts off our backs."

NARRATOR:

What happened?

ANOLITUBBY:

We translated messages and handled telephone calls from the field. The German code experts were flippin' their wigs tryin' to break the new American code. Within 24 hours after our language was pressed into service, the tide of battle had turned. The Allies were on full attack. We were praised by our company commanders and told we'd all get medals.

NARRATOR:

When did you boys receive them?

Audio Direction:

FADE OUT WWII

ANOLITUBBY:

We never did. Turns out the government didn't think we were U.S. citizens, 'cause we are Indians. The Navajo or the Hopi Boys didn't receive any medals for code talking either.

Stage Direction: Simone Anolitubby salutes the audience after her soliloquy. Five seconds.

Claire Cardwell (herself):

In the educational system in the United States, the landing of the Mayflower is taught as one of the most important days in the U.S. history. In WTT's parody of that event, the Indian Chief Who Met The Mayflower, we wanted to show how the dominate culture has written this event to be such a wonderful experience but never does teach Americans how this event affected Native people. No one ever learns that this contact (was it really welcomed?) had a devastating impact the on the communities and even led to some becoming extinct. The Indian Chief Who Met the Mayflower, which Wagonburner members performed, also makes references to the fact that the English who came here were individuals who no one else wanted.

About Princess Wanna Buck:

This scene shows how everyone has made money off the Native culture. In most cases the dominate culture is the one to make the money off our images – not the Native communities. The New Age movement in all parts of the world seems to trivialize the Native culture without having a true in-depth understanding and appreciation for the culture. The scene is written in a very tongue-in-cheek manner, which is very funny onstage.

Jodi Byrd (herself), June 26, 2002:

On "Indian Radio Days" – LeAnne Howe asked members of WagonBurner Theater Troop to write up a little something about our favorite scenes from "Indian Radio Days." I'm not quite sure how to choose, so perhaps a better way to respond to the request is to note all the ways this play is still evolving and still addressing Indian Country and our realities with humor and insight. As I write this during the summer of 2002, I am reading the news and am struck by the degree to which native peoples are still so invisible to the dominant society and its media. Once again as the nation's eyes and media turn their attention towards whatever "national tragedy" they are choosing to focus on this week, they can't even see the forest for the trees, so to speak. And so, even as cameras and reporters descend on towns in Arizona to await the blaze that may or may not obliterate the homes of non-Native people, they don't even see the degree to which these fires are blazing through Apache land or the degree to which local complaints about the Apache nation burning off the underbrush contributed to the fire that is now out of control. It reminds me of a scene from "Indian Radio Days" where an Ojibway man describes a fire that started from a paper mill logging train:

Audio Direction:

FADE UP "WINNEBAGO"

NARRATOR:

I'm am standing in the remains of Cloquet, Minnesota. It is the day after Columbus Day, October 1918. The town and approximately one million acres of the surrounding area have been burned to ash. Sitting on a stump in front of me is an Ojibway man smoking a cigarette. Sir, can you tell us what has happened here?

OJIBWAY INDIAN:

We had a big cookout to celebrate Columbus Day.

NARRATOR (shocked):

You call this a cook-out?

OJIBWAY INDIAN:

Just kidding. (Takes a drag, exhales) Naw, what really happened is a spark from the paper mill logging train started it. You see, before trees turned a profit, us Indians used to burn the undergrowth every year. In some places it made it easier to hunt. Other places it got rid of the bad brush. Let the tall stuff grow better. But seeing as how we got pushed off the land, and no one's been taking care of it. . . . and Kaboom!"

AUDIENCE DIRECTIONS:

Whoop and Holler

Jodi Byrd (herself):

A lot of the scenes from the play still resonate like that for me, and sometimes I think many of these characters from the play like to walk around my head and inject their sharp and occasionally critical observations about the world around us. I mean, what would Jim Montgomery have to say about the state of the Middle East right now? I shudder to think ...

I particularly liked the full-out raucous and sometimes downright nasty humor of the commercials that underscored some of the more serious moments in the play, from the Cheap Brand Cherokee (now Claire, I'm not naming names) to the Big Chief Condoms with Justin in a headdress and armed with a bow and condom. LeAnne does an incredible job hitting home the historical realities even as she deals with all the stereotypes that Indian people still encounter today. I guess if I was pushed, I'd have to say that what appeals to me most about the play, and what I still appreciate about it and LeAnne's work is the willingness not to pull punches, to laugh at everyone and encourage us actors to make fun of ourselves and our experiences as much as we'd laugh at the audience and their expectations.

For me, the best part of doing time with the rest of the WagonBurners was that, for those hours we were rehearsing and on stage performing, I was surrounded by a community of people who shared the same sense of humor, and the same sense of how important it is to capture the perspectives and voices that exist in Indian Country. For a bit of time at any rate, I could forget that I was in Iowa and surrounded primarily by non-Indians. It strengthened my sense of identity and community and for that reason alone, I'll always be glad that I had the opportunity to be a part of the WagonBurner Theater Troop.

Justin Data (himself):

Of course my all-time favorite is:

COMANCHE INDIAN:

(Loudly with terror)

I eat white people for breakfast! I am KO-MAN-CHE!

Another favorite:

AIR is also sponsored by Cheap Cherokee. Nothing runs farther and faster on the road and it won't die on the trail.

One more:

Get off your butts and work off white guilt, as well as build muscles with Jane Fonda's Indian workout special.

And the grand finale!:

NARRATOR:

Ah, I'm standing here on Mars, the so-called Red Planet with Harvey Little Green Man. Harvey is a biotechnician for the Indians in Space Project. Tell me Harvey, how could you Indians, who were once the poorest peoeple in the United States, finance this off-world operation?

HARVEY LITTLE GREEN MAN:

BINGO.

RESEARCH NOTES

THIS BOOK IS BASED ON "Performing Communities: The Grassroots Ensemble Theater Research Project," an inquiry into eight community-based ensemble theaters in the U.S. Conducted by the Community Arts Network (CAN), the project research took place 2000-2001; it was published on the CAN Website in November 2002 at <www.performingcommunities.com>.

The online study lays down a base of 86 interviews with these diverse artist ensembles and their communities, then layers it with comments by the site visitors and critical writing by experts in the field of community-based arts. Also included are theater profiles, photo galleries, play excerpts and documentary resource inventories.

On the "Performing Communities" Website, Robert H. Leonard and Ann Kilkelly provided this information about the project's methodology:

> The findings of the "Performing Communities" project emerged from an extensive process using qualitative research methods and techniques commonly employed in several different fields in the social sciences, humanities and education. The study focused on in-depth interviews with a relatively small set of data. The interviews, field notes and raw data collected by the project site visitors have been coded into categorized topics for analysis. A primary guide for this analytical process was *Qualitative Research for Education: An Introduction to Theory and Methods* by Robert C. Bogdan and Sari Knopp Biklen. This process was

of inestimable value in rendering the volume of perspectives and opinions into useful information to be compared, combined and critiqued.

The methodology of the project also rests on the long-term practice of its leadership and their various sets of approaches to art making – directing and community arts practice, in Leonard's case, and textual analysis and community arts practice in Kilkelly's.

Three questions frame the research project:

1. What does theater rooted in community (or grassroots theater) mean to the participants? (The term "participants" includes everyone involved in the theater experience from conception through performance and subsequent community events.)

2. What do the participants describe as successful practices?

3. What tangible and intangible results happen in the community as a result of the group's work? And, vice versa, what are the effects of the community on the group and its work?

Project Production

"Performing Communities: The Grassroots Ensemble Theater Research Project" was produced by the Department of Theatre Arts at Virginia Tech, under the leadership of Principle Investigator Robert H. Leonard and Co-investigator Ann Kilkelly. The research project was advised by Linda Frye Burnham and Steven Durland of Art in the Public Interest; Annette Markham, Department of Humanities, University of the Virgin Islands; and Katherine R. Allen, Department of Human Development, Virginia Tech. The project was administered by Erica Yerkey.

The materials gathered and written in the project were edited and prepared for online publication by Art in the Public Interest and were published online at the Community Arts Network (CAN) Website. CAN promotes information exchange, research and critical dialogue about and for the field of community-based arts. CAN is headquartered on the World Wide Web at <www.communityarts.net> and is directed by Linda Frye Burnham, Steven Durland and Robert H. Leonard. It is the primary program of Art in the Public Interest.

Art in the Public Interest (API) is a nonprofit organization that provides publications and resources in support of art that is culturally engaged and serving communities. API's goals are to bring about recognition of the arts as part of a healthy culture in which the artist provides both intellectual nourishment and social benefit, and to support art that reflects not only a commitment to quality but a concern for the culture in which that work appears. API is directed by Linda Frye Burnham and Steven Durland. It is based in Saxapahaw, North Carolina.

Project Leadership

Robert H. Leonard, principal investigator

Robert H. Leonard is a professor in the Department of Theatre Arts at Virginia Tech in Blacksburg, Virginia, where he directs the Master of Fine Arts Program in Directing and Public Dialogue. He brings 30 years of experience as founding artistic director of the Road Company, a nationally recognized theater ensemble (1972-1998) based in Johnson City, Tennessee, which created and produced two dozen original plays reflecting the history and issues of the Upper Tennessee Valley and Central Appalachia. Leonard served as a site visitor for WagonBurner Theater Troop for "Performing Communities," and currently serves as a member of the national board of Theatre Communications Group.

Ann Kilkelly, investigator

Ann Kilkelly is a professor in the Department of Theatre Arts and in the Women's Studies Program in the Department of Interdisciplinary Studies at Virginia Tech. She is recognized nationally as a scholar and performer of jazz-tap dancing and history, performance studies and interactive performance techniques. She has received Smithsonian Senior Fellowships and a National

Endowment for the Humanities Collaborative Research Grant, and performs and gives master classes in jazz tap around the country. At Virginia Tech she served as the director of Women's Studies for six years, she teaches and directs multimedia performance concerts, and she recently created the Diversity Training Laboratory to help students and faculty use performance techniques to examine diversity issues. Kilkelly also served as a site visitor for Roadside Theater for "Performing Communities."

Linda Frye Burnham, project editor

Linda Frye Burnham is a writer who is co-director of Art in the Public Interest and the Community Arts Network. She is the editor of APInews and edited "Performing Communities" for the Web and for print. She founded *High Performance* magazine and was its editor 1978-1985, and co-editor 1995-1998. She co-founded the 18th Street Arts Complex and Highways Performance Space in California. She is the editor, with Steven Durland, of *The Citizen Artist: 20 Years of Art in the Public Arena, an anthology from High Performance* (Critical Press, 1998). She has served as contributing editor to the *Drama Review* and staff writer for *Artforum*. Her writing has appeared in numerous art magazines in the U.S. and U.K. She holds an MFA in writing from University of California Irvine.

Steven Durland, project designer

Steven Durland is a visual artist and writer who is co-director of Art in the Public Interest and the Community Arts Network. He served as editor of *High Performance* magazine 1986-1998. He also served as executive director of the magazine's publishing entity, the 18th St. Arts Complex in Santa Monica, California, 1989-1993. He has taught at UC Irvine, lectured at more than a dozen colleges and universities and served on panels at numerous local, national and international arts conferences. His sculpture has been exhibited in New York, Los Angeles, Massachusetts and elsewhere. He holds an MFA in visual art from University of Massachusetts.

Erica Yerkey, project manager

Erica Yerkey worked with the Community Arts Network at Virginia Tech as an administrator from 2000 to 2002, when she left to pursue a graduate degree in Dance/Movement Therapy at Naropa University in Boulder, Colorado. She later rejoined the Network for the CAN Gathering in 2004. A graduate of Radford University, she holds a BFA in contemporary dance. Yerkey has performed and studied with Sara Pearson/Patrik Widrig and Company, Donald McKayle, Bill T. Jones/Arnie Zane Dance Company, the Urban Bush Women, Doug Nielson and the Liz Lerman Dance Exchange among others. She is a teacher, choreographer and performer in her community and elsewhere. Recent residencies include: The Swannanoa Gathering, Virginia Tech Department of Theatre Arts, YMCA Open University, Virginia Tech Women's Center, as well as Radford University.

Site Visitors

Michael Fields, site visitor to Roadside Theater

Michael Fields is a founding member and producing artistic director of the Dell'Arte Company where he acts, directs, teaches, creates plays, manages all company business and oversees development. He is the artistic director of the Dell'Arte Mad River Festival, director of the California State Summer School for the Arts Theatre Program and resident director with Het Vervolg Theatre of Holland. He holds a BA in communication arts from the University of San Francisco and an MFA in directing from Humboldt State University. Fields is on the board of directors of the Theatre Communications Group (TCG) in New York, president of the International Theatre Institute for the USA. He is also a member of the James Irvine Foundation California Arts Leadership Forum, and has served as a National Endowment for the Arts panelist.

Keith Hennessy, site visitor to Jump-Start Performance Co.

Keith Hennessy is an interdisciplinary artist, choreographer, teacher and community arts organizer. He directs Circo Zero, a team of circus, performance and music artists, and his award-winning work has been produced throughout the U.S., and in Canada, Europe, New Zealand and Australia, including several gay/lesbian performance festivals. From 1998-2002, he performed with Cahin-Caha, a French/American cirque bâtard or mongrel circus based in France. Hennessy was a member of the performance collective, CORE, and was a founding member and principle collaborator in Contraband (1985-1994), a dance/performance company directed by Sara Shelton Mann. Hennessy co-founded 848 Community Space (now CounterPULSE), an arts venue in San Francisco. He teaches performance and improvisation internationally and has been on faculty at University of San Francisco, Goddard College Interdisciplinary MFA, New College of California, JFK University and University of California Davis (where he is currently working toward an MFA). Hennessy's Website can be found at <www.circozero.org>.

Ann Kilkelly, site visitor to Roadside Theater
See biography above.

Ferdinand Lewis, site visitor to Cornerstone Theater and Los Angeles Poverty Department
Ferdinand Lewis teaches "Art as a Public Good" in the Public Art Studies Program in the School of Fine Arts at the University of Southern California. He is an Irvine Doctoral Fellow in Urban Planning at the USC School of Policy, Planning and Development, where he has lectured on disaster recovery and community development, methodology and the history of urban form. He has also taught in USC's Urban Neighborhoods program. Lewis served on the faculty of the California Institute of the Arts for nine years, as well as in the California Community Colleges and the California State Summer School for the Arts. He consults in education, urban planning, the arts and community development, and has won four APAC awards for community curricula published by

Los Angeles PBS affiliate KCET. Lewis is the editor of *Ensemble Works: An Anthology* (2005), author of the *Cornerstone Community Collaboration Handbook* (2003), an essayist in *Critical Perspectives: Writings on Art and Civic Dialogue* from Americans for the Arts (2005), and is co-author of *Touch Graphics: The Power of Tactile Design* (2001). He has also written freelance arts journalism for the *Los Angeles Times, Variety, American Theatre* and other publications.

Robert H. Leonard, site visitor to WagonBurner Theater Troop
See biography above.

Arnaldo J. López, site visitor to Teatro Pregones
Born and raised in Puerto Rico, Arnaldo J. López studied English literature, typography and letterpress arts in Pennsylvania, where he also lived and worked as a graphic designer. A Ph.D. candidate in the Department of Spanish and Portuguese at New York University, he writes on issues of identity, arts and politics.

Mark McKenna, site visitor to The Dell'Arte Company
Mark McKenna is artistic director and an ensemble member of Touchstone Theatre, in Bethlehem, Pennsylvania. He is a graduate of the Lecoq International School of Theatre in Paris. He has taught theater classes at Lehigh University and the University of Pennsylvania, and the MFA Theatre Program at Towson State University. McKenna is active in the growth of the Network of Ensemble Theaters. He is a board member of Alliance for Building Communities, a regional community-development corporation.

Nayo Watkins, site visitor to Carpetbag Theatre Company
Nayo Watkins is a poet, essayist, playwright, performer and an arts and community consultant who lives in Durham, North Carolina. She is sole proprietor of Bodacious Consulting and Organizing. She served as coordinator for the Mississippi American Festival Project and for the North Carolina-based

Alternate ROOTS Community Artist Partnership Project. She served as executive director of the African American Dance Ensemble (Durham), At the Foot of the Mountain Theatre (Minneapolis), and the Mississippi Cultural Arts Coalition (Jackson), and as program assistant for the Afro-American Studies Program of the University of Mississippi.

Funding

Support for the Grassroots Ensemble Theater Research Project was provided by Art in the Public Interest, Virginia Tech ASPIRES program, the David and Lucile Packard Foundation, the Open Society Institute, the Nathan Cummings Foundation and the National Endowment for the Arts. Support for this book publication was provided in part by the Nathan Cummings Foundation, the Education Foundation of America and the Rockefeller Foundation.

End Notes

All unattributed citations are from "Performing Communities: The Grassroots Ensemble Theater Research Project" and can be found online at <www.performingcommunities.org>. To locate the context of any material from the study on the Web that is quoted in this book, enter the first few words (with quote marks around them) into the Website's search engine.

The Ecology of Theater-in-Community: A Field Theory

Don Adams and Arlene Goldbard, *Creative Community: The Art of Cultural Development*, New York, Rockefeller Foundation, 2001, p.107.

Linda Frye Burnham, e-mail to the author, 2002.

Marvin Carlson, *Theories of the Theater*, Ithaca, Cornell University Press, 1993, p.317.

Dudley Cocke, "Change: Keynote Address," speech to Kentucky Arts Council conference, October 20, 2000.

Dudley Cocke, personal correspondence with author, June 2002.

Dudley Cocke, Harry Newman and Janet Salmons-Rue, eds., *From the Ground Up: Grassroots Theater in Historical and Contemporary Perspective*, Ithaca, Cornell University, 1993, p.13.

Jan Cohen-Cruz and Lorie Novak, *Urban Ensemble: Univer-*

sity/Community Collaborations in the Arts, New York, New York University Tisch School of the Arts, 1998.

Kathie deNobriga, "An Introduction to Alternate ROOTS," High Performance #64, Winter 1993, p.11.

Sonja Kuftinec, *Staging America: Cornerstone and Community-based Theater*, Carbondale, Illinois, Southern Illinois University Press, Theater in the Americas Series, 2003.

Ruby Lerner, "searching for roots in southern soil," in Kathie deNobriga and Valetta Anderson, eds., *Alternate ROOTS: Plays from the Southern Theater*, Portsmouth, New Hampshire, Heinemann, 1994, p.15.

Barbara Myerhoff, *Number Our Days*, New York, Simon and Schuster, 1978, p. 32.

Richard Schechner, *Environmental Theatre*, New York, Hawthorn Books, 1973, p. 243.

Richard Schechner and Willa Appel, eds., *By Means of Performance: Intercultural Studies of Theatre and Ritual*, Cambridge, Massachusetts: Cambridge University Press, 1990.

Nayo Watkins, interview with the author, April 2002.

Findings: Knowing the Secrets Behind the Laughter

Robert C. Bogdan and Sari Knopp Biklen, *Qualitative Research for Education: An Introduction to Theory and Methods*, Needham Heights, Massachusetts, Allyn and Bacon, Third Edition, 1998.

Cornerstone Theater Company: Love and Respect at Work in the Creative Process

This essay is focused on the processes and approaches for Cornerstone's collaborations in "community shows." The project interviews conducted by Ferdinand Lewis open another, quite wonderful topic: how the Cornerstone ensemble members maintain their own health by periodically creating and producing what they call "ensemble shows." Ensemble members create shows within the ensemble as ways to "stretch muscles" not used in "community shows." Carey and Rauch have very interesting things to observe about how the ensemble uses this and other techniques to maintain and improve company health.

Jump-Start Performance Co.: Magic Glue – The Politics and Personality of Jump-Start

Since this chapter was written, Steve Bailey has stepped down as Executive Director. His title is now Education Director. No one currently holds the title of Executive Director.

WagonBurner Theater Troop: Laughing at the Edge

W.E.B. DuBois, *The Souls of Black Folk: Essays and Sketches*, Chicago: A.C. McClurg & Co, 1903. "Double Consciousness" was a term used by DuBois to describe the experience of the black psyche, "a peculiar sensation. ... One ever feels this twoness – an American, a Negro; two souls, two thoughts, two unreconciled strivings; two warring ideals in one dark body, whose dogged strength alone keeps it from being torn asunder."

Richard Schechner, *Between Theater and Anthropology*, Philadelphia, University of Pennsylvania Press, 1985.

Toni Morrision, *Playing in the Dark: Whiteness and the Literary Imagination*, Cambridge, Massachusetts, Harvard University Press, 1992. "Racialization" is a term used by Morrison to describe images in literary representation that are constructed for African-American people.

Jonathan Swift, "A Modest Proposal for preventing the Children of Poor People from being a Burthen to their Parents or the Country, and for making them Beneficial to the Publick," self-published pamphlet, 1729.

Index

Index

Index

V
Vietnam 10, 35, 61, 65, 104, 172, 177
visual art 117, 125, 155

W
WagonBurner Theater Troop vi, 1, 3, 8,
19, 24, 29, 33, 34, 36, 40, 41, 183,
193-214, 217, 221, 225
Watkins, Nayo 11, 46, 47, 55, 56, 221,
224
Whitehorse, Nancy 41, 199, 201
Wilson, Virgil 135
Woods, Joseph 47

Y
Yerkey, Erica 169, 216, 219
Young Tongues 118

Z
Zettler Family 21
Zollar, Jawole Willa Jo 6

New Village Press

The book you are holding was brought to you through New Village Press, the first publisher to serve the emerging field of community building. Communities are the cauldron of cultural development, and the healthiest communities grow from the grassroots. New Village publications focus on creative, citizen-initiated efforts – "the good news" of social change.

If you enjoyed *Performing Communities* you may be interested in other books we offer about community arts:

Beginner's Guide to Community-Based Arts
A lively comics-illustrated introduction to the work and wisdom of ten activist arts groups. By Mat Schwarzman, Keith Knight, Ellen Forney and others, edited by William Cleveland.

Works of Heart: Building Village through the Arts
A full-color celebration of citizen artists from Oregon to Philadelphia revitalizing their communities.

Upcoming titles include:

New Creative Communities: The Art of Cultural Development
by Arlene Goldbard

Art and Upheaval: Artists at Work on the World's Frontlines
by William Cleveland

Building Commons and Community by the late Karl Linn

The Press is a project of Architects/Designers/Planners for Social Responsibility (www.adpsr.org), an educational non-profit organization working for peace, environmental protection, social justice, and the development of healthy communities.

See what else we publish: **www.newvillagepress.net**

 newvillagePRESS